How To
Feel In Love
And Not Fall For
The Wrong One

In 60 Seconds Or Less

Yvonne L. Jones

Published by
Little Sepia Books Publishing
Copyright © 2018 Yvonne L. Jones
Cover Illustration Copyright © 2018
Little Sepia Books Publishing
All rights reserved.
Cover Illustrator-Richard Svensson
ISBN: 0692729682
ISBN-13: 978-0692729687

DISCLAIMER

I am not a therapist. Reading this book does not create a client-therapist relationship between us. This book should not be used as a substitute for the advice of a competent therapist admitted or authorized to practice in your jurisdiction.

Therefore, any advice, tips, guidelines and instructions contained herein is for awareness purposes only. However, if after reading this book and opting to apply any or all advice offered, the producer of this book will not have a problem accepting some of the credit if you end up with Mr. or Miss Right.

CONTENTS

ACKNOWLEDGMENTS

A big thank you to Nathanial Davis, owner of SWIPE Consulting for providing editorial services. Also, congrats to you sir for recently tying a bow with that special one. Way to go!

A second shout out goes to Ms. E. Conway. Had we not been mauling over the rules of engagement within relationships, the idea for writing a relationship book might not have popped into my head. Thank you, ma'am!

Aside from that seed I just mentioned being planted; this book probably wouldn't have been possible had I not been in a few less then right relationships. Notice I said less than right and not wrong? Yes, I thought you would and no, I'm not sucking up to anyone who might get their feathers ruffled by this book.

Fortunately, I have not been in any dead wrong, could have saved myself the misery had I simply turned around, and ran screaming in the opposite direction the moment we met type of relationships.

Yes, I have been blessed and it wasn't because I was able to escape being in a less than desirable relationship. It was because I learned to recognize one in the making. So, if you're ready to get started, set your stop watch...now!

INTRODUCTION

Where do I begin? Well, it's customary and sometimes logical to start at the beginning. However, doing that will make this introduction larger than the entire book, so I'll begin with you. I will share what I believe this book can do for you *if* you are open to a few suggestions.

First, I would like to remind you of a time when you really didn't have a solid clue about locating the One. However, I'm almost certain it was not from lack of information. You probably received tons of it! More than likely, quite a bit of that information was conflicting. Such as:

"Don't let them know you're interested but do everything to show them that you are!" Really?

Some of the relationship advice you received was sane and relatable, others were questionable. But a few, you absolutely refused to adhere to…ever! Unfortunately, having to muddle through this type of information overload led you right back to square one. One-less!

Then there were those times when you simply threw all caution to the wind. You didn't quite trust your own understanding or judgment, but you were tired of waiting on someone else to give advice you could relate to. So, you took that leap. You leaped but didn't have a clue what you were falling into.

Sure enough, you were swept away, and your heart was broken for your efforts. Sound familiar? Some don't care to admit it, but we've all been there and done that. Well, I don't plan to prolong or exacerbate any disappointment you may still be experiencing. But before you can ever hookup with the One, you must first connect with and know the You.

Ah! I sense this is a concept you've heard of before but

for some reason you didn't adhere to it. You probably minimized or ignored this sage advice because it seemed too easy of a step to make a difference. *Or* maybe you thought it was too difficult of a process to ever complete in your and your desired one's lifetime. It's understandable that you'd love to meet before you both pass over!

Here's the skinny. It has always been up to you as to whether any process will be easy or difficult. There are several things that factor into the ease or complexity one will experience when attempting to accomplish *anything* in life.

I can't say this process will be easy because you'll learn secret short cuts in this book. You will not get any of that here, because you don't need short cuts, tricks or schemes. Besides, I'm not an advocate of those and they won't get you where you desire to be.

Neither will I bait you with the tempting, not to mention unethical lure of the following--that you will be able to avoid all difficulties with this process if you'd simply follow *my* suggestions. On your own and without ever flipping through the pages of this book, it's possible for you to have an "Ah-ha!" moment that will make your process crystal clear.

But until you have that moment, allow me to share the things I've experienced and observed concerning preparing yourself to connect with the One. Just a reminder, I am not a licensed psychologist, psychiatrist, mental health counselor, marriage coach, relationship adviser or any other type of therapist.

However, I'm sure you know that these professionals often have lives that mirror our own. Even though they have extensive clinical and academic knowledge in their field, sometimes they have relationship issues too.

As we so often do, they also get involved with the wrong ones, and ignore or never see the yellow or red warning flags within their relationships. I'm not telling you this to discourage you from seeking professional help. If you feel therapy is the best approach for you, please seek a reputable professional's assistance. I've only mentioned them because I want to bring it to your attention that as learned as they are, they make the same mistakes we do.

They can also decide to become more aware, more aligned with their inner selves and make the necessary adjustments. This is something anyone can do for themselves at any time! But for a few distinctions, we're more alike than not.

As for myself, I'm just a person with an endless curiosity about how to be a better me so that I can experience the fullness of life. My desire to be happy and purposeful has led me to become a note taker, a life stenographer. Taking note and acknowledging that more self-awareness is a definite plus, has helped me improve the quality of my life. Greater awareness will help you do the same.

Therefore, this book is a compilation of both beneficial and conflicting information gleaned, happy and unhappy experiences encountered due to that information, and the eventual wisdom that develops when learning to discern one from the other.

Last but surely not least, you'll learn how to use all this information to your advantage! In this book, I will attempt to persuade you with logical reasons why you should know and trust yourself more. If logic fails to tempt you, then maybe feeling better about yourself will!

You will also learn to recognize blocks—those tall, granite walls of inaccurate beliefs you erect around yourself and maintain without knowing it. With such obstructive or impenetrable walls to breech, the *real* One will find it almost impossible to meet and interact with you!

Note: The real One does not do difficult, neither should you. The question I have for now is this. Will you allow me to share the things I have experienced and observed that can be of benefit to you? If your answer is

"Yes!" then, keep reading!   I'll meet you inside.

.

CHAPTER 1

Going in Circles

We've all been there or will be at some point; all bug-eyed and drooling over someone we just met and who we believe *might* be the one this time. Hold up! Nothing has been checked or verified. So, before anyone gets too carried away, let's just fast forward a few days, weeks or months ahead for the following News flash.

They Are NOT The One!

Now what? Well, most will get right back on that old nag of a horse (ego, wounded pride or biological clock) and limp off into the sunset. Some believe taking Last Ditch Road is the only route left for them to take while in search of their elusive other half.

Then there are those who will take the secluded route, the Tuck Tail N Run Expressway which happens to exit at Hell No Never Again Boulevard. And many will continue to travel on Loop 360, revisiting the same type of dead-in relationships they always have.

Fortunately, some will decide to take a ride on that recently opened highway. Unfortunately, not enough of us consider taking this new route--Reassessment Interchange. This is a highway uncluttered by distracting or misleading claims or false self-promotions and has no confusing change over or exit lanes. You know exactly where it's taking you and how to get on or off it!

Reassessment Interchange always has little to no traffic with designated slow, moderate and highspeed lanes. This enables one to move at their own pace. Any road construction or maintenance is done well after peak hours. Scheduling improvements or upkeep apart from peak traffic hours helps to impede the occurrence of relationship backups and accidents.

Do any of these routes sound familiar to you? I'm sure some of them do since you have traveled one or two of these highways or byways a few times yourself. But right about now, if you've been "on the chase" for a bit, you're probably feeling a lot like Wile E Coyote.

Why? Because you keep convincing yourself that running in circles, scheming, begging, praying and getting hurt in the process is a worthy sacrifice *if* it results in you nabbing the winner's prize--the One.

Well, Wile E never figured it out, but you don't have to run yourself ragged chasing someone you can never catch, trip up, out run or trick into a committed relationship in the first place.

Wile E will never catch his prize--the Road Runner, because unbeknownst to him it has been written in the script that way. There's also the possibility of you never catching your prize because *you* keep writing your script to play out in the same way.

Wouldn't it be easier to learn how to write a better script, one which ends with both of you being winners? Shouldn't a co-creative relationship be structured around a win-win scenario for *both* parties? If you agree, then to make this happen, you'll have to let go of any one-sided, unproductive concepts or ideas concerning nabbing potential ones.

Especially if what's required of you is the use of costly, time consuming tricks, tactics or traps like the ones implemented by the crafty and ingenious Wile E. I think you already know the use of subterfuge and schemes is not only dishonest but demonstrates a lack of true concern or love for the other party. You are not Special Ops on a mission to seek out enemy combatants!

Remember, this is about love and not about in-house fighting or strategizing. Within the confines of love all *is* fair, but not with war. With war, there is the perception of one winner. That is, if you can call the one who reaps the spoils of war a winner. There is also the perception of one loser, the one who loses or forfeits a thing once possessed.

But what if the thing lost or forfeited was no longer deemed beneficial or desired by the designated loser? Do you think they'd consider not having possession of a thing they no longer desire to be a loss? No. If not for the destructive act of war, they would probably thank you for taking yourself off their hands!

How do you think the self-proclaimed winner would feel knowing that the relationship they exerted so much energy to acquire, was deemed no more valuable than a tattered rag tossed in a filthy trash can? They may never admit it, but more than likely they'd feel very, very foolish.

Just as with any war between nations, relationship wars can require enormous amounts of emotional, physical and financial investments. When the war is over and the blood, sweat and tears have finally settled, both parties will probably be delighted to come away with their shirts somewhat intact!

War on any front is a precious waste of energy, resources and quality of life. No one is truly a winner as there can be much to lose and even less to gain. However, if you somehow find yourself neck deep within the trenches of a full-scale, War of the Roses type of relationship, it's possible for you to recoup some if not most of your losses.

There's always the option of negotiating a truce, sincerely letting bygones be bygones, setting new boundaries and dropping some borders. *Or* if all else fails, try raising that unblemished, white flag of surrender.

Hold up, before you start screaming, *"I am NOT surrendering NOTHING!"* Allow me to explain what I mean. Surrendering does not entail you lying down and getting steamrolled by another. Surrendering begins to happen when one becomes courageous enough and chooses to be a more aware, loving and balanced person.

It means giving up those knee jerk responses to accuse, judge and convict others and yourself. It means no more emotional game playing, no more tit-for-tat, no more guilt trips, no more terminal thinking and no more spiteful speaking. It also means allowing others to be who they are—warts and all!

Now, I didn't say you must continue kicking it with them as you are surrendering all *your* negative stuff. You will have to continue releasing those unbeneficial aspects of yourself whether you opt to kick it with them or not!

On paper, surrendering looks like a lot, doesn't' it? That's because it is. It's a lot of letting go! *But* don't be fooled by the letting go part, because it will not always be easy. Surrendering, letting go is quite often an uncomfortable process for most people. It can be a slow, sometimes tedious progression as there's no way one can instantly release every bit of negativity in their life.

However, if we by-pass developing greater awareness and self-empowerment, we will continue to repeat the mishaps and miss those successes in life we'd love to experience. When facing pivotal or tough times, it's essential that we become more aware and deeply vested in the belief that better, more uplifting solutions exist.

"Okay, I agree that being more aware and avoiding a war is best. But please tell me why the heck am I reading a book that's not going to give me tips and tricks for catching the right one?"

I know *you* didn't ask that question after what I just said about tricks and traps but just in case some are wondering the same thing, here's why.

Unless you equate that special one to a cold, a fish or a bag of tricks, you may find it difficult to lure, hook, catch *or* sleight of hand them. Oh, you can try but it's unlikely that you'll end up with the fantastic results you are seeking.

Sidebar: Technically, you don't catch a cold. Colds have perfected invading the body, overwhelming its defenses and making it difficult for the one invaded to gain control over their own body! I'm sure this is not the outcome you're seeking when dealing with viruses *or* relationships.

Now, if you're relating your potential Ones to the proverbial abundant numbers of fish in the sea, there are several diverse types of them you must become aware of. Just as you are, certain fish are exclusively attracted to certain lures.

Baiting your hook with a lure they're not the least bit interested in, can result in them either ignoring or quickly swimming away from you. Naturally, some will be daring enough to venture where others will not. They will test your lure *and* take a bite.

However, after a brief or exhaustive struggle to reel them in, you may find that you'll have to toss them back. Why? Because the fish you caught does not meet *your* specifications at all!

Even if you're using the right lure, if you are deep fishing far beneath unfamiliar murky waters, prior to pulling your catch up and inspecting it, there's no way to know what you've hooked. It could be you've captured a big annoying megamouth, a stubborn bullheaded hammerhead, *or* some other undesired deep-water creature you can't relate to and have no idea what to do with *except* to throw it back!

The bag of tricks is even more troublesome to get a handle on, as you may be required to enroll in magician school. But be aware--any sleight of hand, under the table use of mirrors, pulleys, springs or smoke will probably be useless. Remember, that "bag of tricks" you're attempting to amuse already knows the same tricks you do, and maybe more!

So, what's a body to do with so much pressure coming from all over the place concerning finding the best One for them? Some believe they must contend, make amends or go along with the outer pressures forced on them by family and friends. Whether well-meaning or not, these types of instigators will stress the need for you to be more expedient when it comes to finding the One.

Their concern is that you're getting too old to continue missing the mark. Neither will it be beneath them to make unsubstantiated remarks about the family's bloodline ceasing to exist if you continue to do so. Of course, this imminent annihilation of family will all be due to your lack of substantial contribution. Therefore, they will also insist that *your* One be someone they will be proud to acknowledge as a member of the family.

Receiving a family membership usually requires one to possess the appropriate character traits, to have a certain level of success in life *and* the lineage to back all that up! Sometimes these memberships are meticulously doled out by the matriarch or patriarch of the family. However, just like high-end stock options, if you're unable or unwilling to pay the price, they are almost impossible to acquire.

As you may already know, family is not always the thorn in your side. Total stranger will feel it is their benevolent contribution to the world to first point out your unfortunate One-less status. They will then go on to give you detailed or sketchy instructions about how to fix it—as if you're blind, baffled *and* broken. Case in point:

Unsolicited Advice #101: *"Obviously you don't have a man or else he'd be here changing this flat tire for you. Get you a man who knows how to keep your car in tiptop shape. Every woman should have someone to...blah, blah-blah, blah-blah..."* Yeah, this advice was directed at me.

Unsolicited Advice #102: *"Don't you get tired of restaurant food? Eating out is expensive too. You need to find a woman who cooks!"* A good friend of mine reported this one.

Do you see what I mean about unsolicited advice coming out of the woodwork? Outside of family and friends, you never see it...or maybe I should say see *them* coming. Even if you could, what would be the best non-combative response to someone's unrequested and more than likely inappropriate advice?

Sure, you may have chosen and then paid Your Flat We Fix Tire Service, who then saw fit to dispatch Mr. Jackedup to your rescue. But I bet you had no idea relationship counseling came with your emergency roadside service. I certainly didn't. Likewise, I'm willing to bet no one intentionally orders Deep Fried Insult as their main course, and subsequently pays for the privilege of being told their food choice is not the smartest.

If that doesn't give you indigestion or cause your stomach to rumble, how about having an unrecognizable, under-cooked slice of the house special? The No Surprise You're Still Single crumb cake dropped in front of you with about as much fanfare as a dirty ashtray! Doesn't look *or* smell very appetizing, does it?

Trust me; I so understand how annoying uninvited advice can be. How well do I recognize the temptation to drop Mr. Jackedup with a crowbar to the back of the knee? Not to mention the sweet release of Ninja tossing a plate at Ms. Tactless, the rarely tipped waitress! Yes, I know those feelings very well.

Imagining yourself yielding to these temptations can feel euphoric. However, I will advise against catering to those urges. Unless you're okay with having the one in the black robe sitting on that high bench, looking down at you and saying:

"I'm giving you three meals and a cot for your trouble."

Before you can even begin to register what just happened, the judge's verdict is quickly followed by a huge man in arms who escorts you to your new time out spot! Yes, I'm being comical but if we are to be honest with ourselves, there are times when we must learn to swallow our indignation whether it is righteous or not.

When we take an unbiased look at a previous or current "advisory committee's" suggestions, we may come to realize a few things. One is that there may have been a tiny grain of truth hidden within the dreaded unsolicited advice received. The other thing is, once we sincerely take note of that tiny grain or huge boulder of truth, that awareness can be the catalyst which prompts us to look deeper within. For instance, paying closer attention to how we feel about certain situations or conditions affecting our lives.

Just a note, *all* things affect your life in some way. But once you begin paying closer attention to what and how you're feeling, it will be easier to understand the necessity for making changes or adjustments when needed.

Paying attention and checking inward is the one habit you should hone to near perfection. Doing so will aide you in every aspect of your life. But since we're discussing the subject of relationships, let's apply this habit to that.

Implementing this powerful habit can spare you from experiencing unnecessary pain and grief. You will be more willing and able to correctly assess whether there are self-issues that should be addressed and resolved *before* attempting to connect with the One in the first place!

How can you even began seeking the perfect One when *you* are out in left field, and nowhere near the perfect One for *them*? Do you really believe anyone with a few brain cells firing off will want to get into a serious, life-changing relationship with someone who's **not** dealing with any of their own issues? No, you don't.

It's a good thing we are each endowed with an internal system that can assist us in making sound decisions about anything in life. Let's just call it our unique internal radar and navigational system.

This system is comprised of an inner intuitive switchboard. Among other things, it acts like a helpline and provides the insight that allows us to quantify those *"Ah ha!"* moments. It also consists of gauges that monitor and allow adjustments to any emotional triggers we may activate or deactivate.

All the intuitive and sensory signals we receive is monitored by this specialized and individually designed navigational system. When we allow it to, it helps us determine if we're on the right track or lost somewhere.

Unfortunately for some, their navigational system is often overlooked. Because we don't always understand exactly how we work, those internal checks and balances (we recognize these as our feelings, emotions, thoughts and flashes of insight) are either ignored or perceived to be our imagination at play.

Let's look at the alarm of discomfort or pain. We usually instantly opt to take something that will numb or cover up the pain. Often, we bypass checking our internal monitors to determine the underlying reason for the discomfort or pain we're feeling.

Pain alarms can be triggered by something as simple as stressing over an event that is scheduled to happen in the future. I'm sure you know how it goes. For whatever the reason, you decide to stress about an upcoming date and because you do, your muscles get all knotted up.

The muscle groups that knot up are those in your traps and neck, which then precede to cause tension headaches. This type of pain in the neck (pun intended) can easily be remedied. When you start paying closer attention to your internal switchboard, you can better monitor and regulate your thoughts and emotions. By doing so you can easily discover what's really causing you pain and correct it!

Sometimes all it takes is the awareness of what you are doing that's facilitating pain. Once you know, then you can simply do the opposite. In this instance, it would benefit you to stop stressing. No pharmaceuticals required! However, a trip to a masseuse or sauna would be wonderful!

Think about this. If you've done all that you know to do concerning this future date, what good will stressing about it do *besides* be a pain in your neck or some other part of your anatomy? It's possible to adjust or remove feelings of pain, unworthiness, failure, fear, doubt or any of the other things we feel or believe to be true but are usually not.

Let's apply the notion that men should not be as sensitive as women. Most men are instructed to:

"Man up, never let them see you sweat, and you'd better not ever let them see you cry!"

Following this set of instructions to the letter means that a man's only option is to behave like an insensitive, unemotional zombie or bully, *and* that they are not truly of the male gender if they don't follow it! Man, that's so untrue and unfair!

Men are human and endowed with the same ability for emotional release as women. By the way, releasing is much healthier then penning emotions up or denying them. Men also come with sweat glands and tear ducts, and they should utilize those glands and fluids whenever they need to!

The same crazy and equally irrational instructions extend to women as well. I'm assuming those who craft these instructions only want to be fair about it. Men and women should suffer equally. Therefore, women are instructed to:

"Never let them see how smart and capable you really are, doing that only intimidates them. Cry every now and then and pretend you need help when you don't. In this way, everyone feels useful!"

Do I really need to dismantle this asinine instruction with a response? No, I refuse to do that, but I will state the obvious. When vital information to our well-being is misinterpreted, ignored or erroneously given and then acted on, an imbalance occurs. If this imbalance is not corrected, we will eventually become off-centered. *But* we can fine-tune and even upgrade our awareness skillset, a.k.a. understanding. This is great news! Whether we go willingly or drag ourselves along while kicking and screaming, we are always in a learning process.

How many times have you upgraded your phone or computer and had to figure out how to use it? What about the new car you bought after riding around in your familiar old hooptie for several years?

Since you may have opted to by-pass the thick user's manual that came with your new computer, phone or car, it probably took a bit of head scratching before you could properly setup a new audio program or radio channels to your specifications.

When you're dealing with something new and different, you can't apply the same old thinking or knowledge. Not if you expect it to work or be as useful as it is designed to be. Most of the problems we face in life come about because we try to get around learning. We'd much rather find a short cut for the process. Or as you already know, sometimes we flat out refuse to learn—as if we're hurting somebody else! Really?

Refusing to learn does not mean the learning process simply goes away. Sorry, that ain't happening! It's still there, patiently waiting for you to initiate and then customize your unique learning process.

But again, you can do so at any time. It's never too soon or too late to learn. It is entirely up to you whether it takes the blink of an eye, a steady and progressive pace, years until you have that flash of insight *or* if you never get it!

Come on now, you must admit that making a few adjustments is far better than incurring jail time. It also beats the heck out of running around in circles without ever getting anywhere. *Or* hiding how you feel and being afraid to learn the things you are truly capable of accomplishing in life!

Besides, relying on overly tried and unsuccessful techniques tends to become discouraging, even depressing over time. Most will simply give up or accept any ole one who shows up. Which when you think about it is even more depressing.

From your current perspective, it may seem as if you are nowhere near your desired destination--on a lush, tropical oasis where you're pampered and catered to by the love muffin of your dreams! But don't stress or give up because you're not there yet. Instead, try cutting yourself some slack and giving yourself more credit.

You *are* looking at other options. This is the reason you're here. And think about it. It's almost impossible for *anyone* to see clearly when they're stuck idling in soul numbing, mind-traffic, or looping around the frustrating road construction going on inside of their head.

Once you begin moving beyond your self-imposed grid lock, you'll come to realize that you are much closer to meeting that special someone than you ever imagined. So, here are just a few of my recommendations.

Be patient, give yourself time to adjust and grow, stop stressing so much, let go of your fears, live your life to the fullest while you're in this learning process *and* never, ever give up on connecting with that special One!

If you do this, not only will you rock the 60 second count down that's coming in a later chapter, you will be positioning yourself to becoming that awesome One *your* special One is seeking as well!

You did know that you were not the only one seeking to make this life enriching connection, right? Of course, you did! It's the reason you're getting prepared and hopefully you're not under the assumption of their being only one potential One for you in life either.

If that were the case, most of us would never hook up with any One! God, the universe, life itself is too immense for you to think on such a small scale. As a matter of fact, I'll need you to up your thinking game as you continue to peruse this book.

There are unlimited probabilities of there being numerous Ones just for you! If you miss one opportunity, then rest assured there will be others. They may not be exactly like the one you think you've missed out on, but there's absolutely no reason why they can't be a better One!

A better one coming along means you upped your game and became a better you! If you desire better, then you won't shy away from becoming that awesome, bodacious being you've kept tucked away all this time. Okay, I don't want to overwhelm you before we even begin the process. So, let's get started!

CHAPTER 2

Your Radar Isn't Broken It's Just Off!

Picture this. Your city, present day and you're walking down a crowded street, shopping at the mall or visiting your favorite place of worship. Then suddenly and out of nowhere appears, *"I just might be the One!"*

You are keenly aware of your internal radar tracking device as it locks on target and zooms in like a pair of high-tech, fully functional cybernetic eyes. That radar of yours pulls up their stats almost instantly! To certify what you hope you're seeing, you move in closer, pull up your mental list of physical traits you've insisted the One should have and begin checking them off one by one:

"Height, check! Weight, check! Attire, check! Swag, check! Eye contact, check! Smile, check! Sex appeal, check! Smells great, check! Checks me! Check!"

And just when you think it can't get any better than this, the thing that confirms it for you suddenly appears just above their head in flashing, bold, neon colored lights:

Target *"The One"*
LOCATED!!

Of course, no one will blame you for *not* being able to ignore all of that! But doesn't this sound exactly like the way many of us locate a potential one? Also, does it seem we go a bit insane when we meet someone and *everything* about them seems perfect to us?

Sure, we've only known them for a hot minute, but during that moment and in our mind, those sizzling sixty-seconds feels like a lifetime! We've already exchanged names, rings, addresses and relatives without ever leaving the room *or* asking one pertinent question like, *"Are you single?"*

We're so wrapped up in the shiny packaging until we forget about the actual gift hidden beneath the fancy gift wrap. You already know what happens when we *assume* what's inside will match what is being reflected on the outside. The two often fail to complement one another, which may or may not be a dreadful thing.

Please don't misunderstand me. I am not saying all packaging is false advertisement. However, one would be remiss to ignore what lies beneath. We tend to either underestimate or over-rate the packaging and doing either can be a grave mistake.

Let's say you routinely purchase cookies during your favorite organization's yearly cookie drive. You've been doing so for years and never had a problem with the product or the kids selling them. You know the kids are not always in uniforms when selling, but they always have the appropriate forms and trademark designed boxes of cookies.

One evening your door bell rings and you answer it. There standing before you is the cutest little girl! She's accompanied by an older teenager who looks like her sister.

Neither are wearing uniforms, but you know exactly who they are and why they're ringing your bell. Those familiar boxes of cookies stacked inside the little cart they're pulling tells you all there is to know.

They are the very same cookies you purchase every year. And because they only have a few boxes left, you decide to help them out and purchase all five of them. You have no intentions of eating all those cookies, so you save one for you and your family and give the others away to friends and co-workers.

But not even an hour after giving those cookies away, you get reports of the boxes containing crackers instead of the cookies displayed on the box! You're dumb founded because you know this organization doesn't sell crackers. There's a slim to no chance crackers got mixed up with cookies at the processing plant.

Then the light bulb comes on. You were an unsuspecting victim of fraud and there was no way you could have avoided it! Well...maybe there was but remember, this is just a hypothetical example of how we can be misled by packaging.

So, please continue to support the girls with their cookie sales! I have supported them for many years, and I've seen nothing that will change that. I merely used the example of cookie sales to make a valid point about the things we can become so accustomed to and never question.

However, there are some things most of us would *never* do without deeper introspection or extensive fact checking. For instance, would you make the snap decision to allow a stranger--someone you just met moments ago, to take care of your beloved child, pet or home? Would you base your decision on how well dressed and in fashion they are, by the type of car they pull up in or from what they tell you concerning their aptitude for the job? I certainly hope not, and yet this is exactly what a lot of us do when it comes to certifying the One. We don't!

Remember the movie Mrs. Doubtfire? In the movie Robin Williams plays a father who takes extreme measures to *look* like a capable female housekeeper and nanny. The father's packaging and spot on responses to every inquiry is so convincing that he fools everyone.

Not only did he fool his ex-wife, a smart and capable woman he was married to for many years, but his children *and* employer too! It's a hilarious, funny and loveable family movie. If you haven't seen it, you should.

However, the fallout that occurs because of the father's elaborate and false advertisements, though comical for viewers to witness, could have been disastrous for a real-life off-screen family. Had he *not* been a loving, protective father and ex-husband whose only desire was to have more quality time with his kids, life for his children and ex-wife could have become the stuff horror stories are made of.

I won't go into details concerning the rest of the movie, but what if he had been the absolute opposite of his outer disguise/presentation? Unbeknownst to the mother, she would have allowed a wolf to watch over her lambs, and it goes without saying that she could have placed herself in grave danger as well.

A scenario such as this one occurring sounds extreme, and yet it happens all the time. We get broadsided by what on initial glance *looks* like the answer to our prayers. Because we are so thankful for the golden Trojan gift we are presented, we invite it into our encampment with open arms and without further inquiry.

One would think that in today's now you see it now you don't, hocus-pocus brand of advertising, people would be a bit more inquisitive. Or that the acceptance of anything at face value would be placed on hold to allow for further scrutiny. Unfortunately, this is not always the case.

We have become a *"Give it to me right now no matter the cost!"* instant self-gratifying society. If we can gain access to something by yesterday, then the initial cost doesn't seem to matter very much. That is, until the next day. Tomorrow's pain is when the true price we've paid for any quickly attained, inferior, overly hyped *and* priced, assembly-lined knock-off "goods" no longer looks or feels like the best trade off.

Sometimes it's long past the morning after when we realize that waiting a bit longer for goods made from quality, time tested, natural (real) materials, that have been produced with the highest level of craftsmanship and backed by an authentic seal of approval *with* a lifetime warranty included is far better!

Yes, I do realize that was a very long sentence, but it was my soapbox speech. Good thing for me *you* are patient enough to allow me my say. However, for now I'm stepping off the box. But doesn't this strike you as odd? Especially when considering all the advantages top quality goods can offer, why is it so many willingly choose inferior ones instead?

Well, when one's radar setting is off kilter and they don't know it, then it's very easy to miss what seems apparent to others. That a quickly acquired inferior thing is not better than or equal to a patiently awaited, higher quality thing.

We all know of a friend, family member or maybe someone a little closer to home (yes…this could be you) who seems to end up with the wrong person of interest repeatedly. If you ever ask them why they keep choosing someone who is totally wrong for them, they'll probably give this response:

"I don't know why! They just seem to keep popping up. It's almost like they're following me around!"

Their assumption of being followed around is correct. But they are highly mistaken in believing the wrong ones are simply stumbling upon them by chance. Nothing could be further from the truth. They're being followed because *they* are the ones broadcasting *their* location to the wrong ones! I can just hear what you're wondering right now.

"Come on Yvonne how is it they don't know that?"

I'll just follow up with my own question. Did you know it when *you* did it? Exactly! Most of us never see ourselves as beacons for disaster because we have been led to believe we are handling the situation in the best conceivable way.

To this day, most young or ~~older~~ *seasoned* women and even men are told they must find someone to share the joys and burdens of life. The emphasis is on them doing so sooner as opposed to later. The reasoning behind this type of grab somebody while you can approach, most likely stems from the notion that becoming a fully developed individual could take forever! And it's not something you want to do alone. Remember, what we don't have is a whole lot of time.

Because we fear that time is of the essence, we tend to make things even more confusing and complicated for ourselves. Some hold the belief or hope that two unaware and clueless individuals within a relationship can somehow manage to help each other develop in key areas of life.

But since they are each so unaware, how do they move past their current level and what can they possibly develop besides more cluelessness? Don't answer that! It was a rhetorical question. Clearly, two unaware or clueless individuals will find it extremely difficult to nurture a stable, dynamic relationship. That is, unless at least one of them (best case scenario—both) wakes up and gets a clue from somewhere!

But just in case there's too little awakening or clue finding going on, to help us wrap this process up even quicker, we are cautioned not to be too picky. After all, no one is perfect. One just might have to settle for the next best thing.

I'm sure you're wondering what the next best thing is? Well, that usually turns out to be someone less than perfect for you! I don't know, maybe I'm missing something vital with that lowered expectation concept. But in my opinion, that dog just doesn't hunt! Following *that* dog nullifies the point of desiring to meet the One--i.e., the best one for you.

Here's something else to think about. How is it that some can so quickly or eventually settle for not just less but the absolute *opposite* of what they desire? Is it because they believe their best match is not meant for them, since they have failed to quickly materialize?

Or, is it they feel undeserving of experiencing that which is desired and that settling for less or the opposite will somehow someday make them happy? But how does that happen when one has already envisioned better! Accepting less usually comes with deep regrets, yet we often do just that—we settle.

Some will even attempt to minimize or to forget whatever it is they once desired. I must admit that permanently forgetting what is desired but unattained would be a neat trick. It's a technique some would pay handsomely to learn.

Except, short of remaining in a drug induced stupor or having a disease or injury to the brain, it's virtually impossible to unknow what you already know you desire to

experience. Once that genie gets out the bottle, it's out!
I'm sure you've known or heard of a couple who appeared to be very happy and stayed together for many years.

However, as soon as their children were grown and out of the house and to the dismay of everyone who knew them, they separated. When asked why they made the decision to separate after so many years of seemingly blissful cohabitation, one or both may state the following:

1. They simply grew apart.
2. Somehow over time they'd completely lost that loving, caring feeling for the other.
3. From the very beginning, one or both held and maintained deep reservations about the union.

Under pretense, some will spend decades in a relationship neither is truly happy with. Yes, there are many valid reasons couples have for staying together despite them growing apart, or no longer loving each other. Sometimes they believe it's better for their children if they stay together. They may stay together for financial and cultural reasons, or social status. Even the fear of some unknown disaster somehow shattering what they have built together, is a strong deterrent against separation.

Apparently, these types of arrangements are accepted by one or both parties all the time. But it's difficult for me to wrap *my* mind around accepting these reasons for getting into or remaining in a less than co-creative relationship.

I simply can't see myself **not** loving the one I choose to spend a significant amount of intimate time with. Neither can I envision being in a co-creative relationship in which from the very beginning there was never the intention of being an intimate, resonating partner.

How does it benefit either when one is not being honest about their feelings, thoughts, reservations or concerns within the relationship? Do some attempt to suppress their feelings and desires because it is believed they must grab any undesired yet conveniently available person with an interest in *them*? Can this be the reason we too often anticipate and accept such dismal relationships? If so, how does one begin to change their acceptance of such meager expectations?

If change is to occur, if happiness and peace from within is to become the expected norm, then at some point we must each come to terms with and resolve these ageless questions. We cannot continue to ignore or wish them away. Future bloodlines might be at stake!

I know, it was so wrong of me to tease you about your bloodline possibly falling into the abyss. However, by now I'm sure you understand that you can't keep following the same old advice if it keeps giving you the same undesired results. If said advice hasn't worked so far, more than likely it never will. But I believe you already know this because you're still here with me now, and it's not because I'm such a persuasive or entertaining writer.

No, you're here because you're looking for a sane method that will give you the lasting results you are seeking. A method that will help you experience a more loving, co-creative relationship with another of like mind and heart. You are not looking for the same things anymore, you're ready to upgrade!

Hopefully, you're beginning to sense that I may have something more to offer you that will help. It just depends on how open (not gullible) and receptive you are to change. However, I do realize that some of the advice you have received over the years came from people you know, love

23

and trust a whole lot more than you do me. Heck…you don't even know me yet!

Because you are looking elsewhere for advice concerning such a sensitive matter, it may feel as if you are rejecting theirs in some way. Don't entertain that thought because you are not. What you *are* doing is accepting the fact that you desire to experience more, and you will no longer hold yourself back. You're simply looking at some options.

It has nothing to do with rejecting another, but everything to do with you accepting *your* desire to broaden and strengthen your self-awareness and growth potential. Maybe you can think about it in this way. If those you love and respect, love and respect you in return they will be thrilled that you have decided to grow even more in love and awareness. They will be the first one's in your cheering section!

They'll honor and respect the process you choose to follow because it is entirely up to you as to how and when you progress in life. It is not a decision they can make or carry out for you. Sure, they may not understand or agree with every part of your process. However, if what you do is coming from genuine love of self and others, then eventually they will notice a wonderful change in you. A change for the better and not the worse. Now, why would they have any objections to that?

Better yet, your expanding awareness will enable you to see why incorporating other's desperate approach to love and companionship is not the least bit helpful. Some of those desperate methods will cost you more money, time and sanity then you'll care to lose!

If you elect to implement and understand that this will be an ongoing process in your life, you will better learn the importance of dealing with yours, and then others disempowering concepts right away. How do you deal with others disempowering concepts? Easy, by not making them yours!

It's never a clever idea to co-mingle other's unresolved issues with your own. It's a given that you will have to come to terms with *your* own fears, doubts, insecurities and misunderstandings before you can help anyone else come to terms with there's.

Remember, whether it's physical, mental or spiritual growth, it takes time. Therefore, this is a process you cannot rush. One of the reason's it takes time for us to grow is that we need to build up our self-confidence, understanding and love.

There will be some life lessons that you will understand and utilize immediately. You'll get them right away! Then there will be some in which you will have to revisit several times before you even have an inkling as to what they mean, and how you should apply them in your life.

Don't rack your brain trying the figure out why this is so. It is what it is. You can't know what you don't know until you know it! We are often very impatient and will try to side-step, leap over or tunnel under that perceived "block of time" needed for gaining more awareness. But the only thing all that avoidance activity does is to add even *more* time to the process!

Somehow, we fool ourselves into believing we can expedite receiving the benefits associated with higher awareness. However, that expectation is pure fallacy. When one has yet to improve or increase upon their current level of awareness, how can they expect to receive anything different or better than before? Well that's a no brainer, they can't! Remember that clueless couple? I rest my case.

Neither is it a mystery when we end up feeling miserable, lost and desperate at times. When we put little-to-no effort into understanding how our dreams and goals can come about, we get very little if any value out of that no-effort approach. If you invest nothing into it, you get more of the same out of it!

Some will place more value on their possessions/things, then they do on themselves or other people. Now, how does *that* ever happen? Though we often wonder why or how things come about, most of us have witnessed first-hand what happens when a person gets lost and becomes desperate.

We become the unfortunate witnesses to their poor choices in life. Sometimes those choices are deadly ones. So, is it any wonder why an unaware, insecure, self-doubting, fearful and desperate person will choose the wrong other half time and time again? Especially when they haven't fully invested in *their* half of the equation!

Now don't go working yourself into a tizzy! I am not saying you are a lost cause, and that you exhibit all the character traits I just mentioned. But you can't deny that you do have an affinity for one or two of them, and maybe some others I didn't mention.

Question. Can growing in awareness ever happen if one is afraid of their own unique growth process? That was another suggestive question--the answer is self-evident. But please indulge me for just a moment more. I'd like to share the following parable with you which relates to self-awareness and growth. I've titled it *The Poison Within:*

A man becomes lost in the desert and has been without provisions for several days. Eventually a well-equipped traveler comes along, sees that the man is in trouble and offers to share water from his canteen. However, the man's state of severe dehydration has caused him to become confused. The water which will surely save his life, is perceived to be a poison that will end it.

The traveler knows the man is not thinking clearly and tries to convince him the water is safe to drink. To prove it, he takes three sips of water and swallows it. Still, the man refuses to drink. He then comes up with valid reason after reason why the lost man should drink, but to no avail.

Briefly, he considers forcing the man to drink but decides against it. Because they are miles away from the next watering hole, he can't risk wasting one drop of it. He doesn't mind sharing it, but he will not watch it evaporate into the hot desert sand.

In hopes that he may eventually persuade the parched man to drink, he decides to wait for him to calm down from his agitated state. He does relax and appears to doze off but has died from thirst. The traveler felt genuine concern for this man who was so consumed with the fear of a possible death, until he could not see the life he already held within his grasp.

What do you believe was the lost man's poison? Was it unpreparedness, his misconceptions or illusions concerning his circumstances? How about fear or lack of trust? Would greater awareness have neutralized any one of the lost man's poisons and thereby saved and enriched his life?

If we don't really know who we are and what we're truly capable of accomplishing, we can become lost in many ways. Within a state of delusion, some will wander within their own personal desert for years.

They no longer recognize the things they once desired or knew to be beneficial. Because of their lost state of being, the best things for them could land gently in the palm of their hand, only to be discarded or cast away by them.

Do you better understand how awareness, or the lack thereof affects every aspect of your life? By now, I'm hoping you do and herein lies the best reasons for upgrading your internal radar!

Your upgraded radar is equivalent to an extremely efficient, specialized, multi-functioning, quantum, bio-tool. Think of it as combined Radar, GPS and AI which means **Advanced** Intelligence, because there's nothing artificial about it! Also, your radar possesses discernment, benevolence and love, but has no moving parts to wear out. Infinite upgrades are included as well!

The unequaled degree of precision in an upgraded radar is mind blowing awesomeness! And the best thing about it is it won't cost you one copper penny because you can't buy it. You can only build or upgrade it using the elements you already possess!

Once you've assembled it to your unique specifications, you must then get in sync with it if it is to better assist you in life. Most definitely, when you're done recalibrating it, you'll have to turn it on *and* pay attention!

Who wants to get caught in a relationship, debt, scarcity, people pleaser or any of those other traps in life? Oh wait, I forgot to mention the most prevalent and underestimated one, the impatient, *"I have to have it right now!"* speed trap!

CHAPTER 3

Undressing the Wizard

If you equip your car with a radar detector, will the device steer you in the right direction or help you avoid traffic like GPS? No, it will not. The standard radar's only function or purpose is to help you detect upcoming speed traps. Then you can slow your roll, adjust your speed and avoid getting a ticket.

However, having this nifty device does not negate the need for awareness. If you fail to turn it on, or if you are *not* paying attention and miss your radar's warning signal, you will roll right up to the very person you intended to avoid.

Who might that be you ask? That person is the problematic, overly pretentious one most of us know as Mister or Miss PoPo! So how is it that a PoPo can pick you out of a crowd, and how do you squeeze by with just a warning? Here's how you get got or not! It depends on the following:

1. How fast you are moving. PoPo's are usually not very interested in slow or careful rollers. They know it's harder

for you to spot them when you're moving too fast. However, they will make exceptions to this rule.

2. The make and model of the vehicle you're operating. Are you operating a vehicle with a flashy designer paint job, shiny name brand rims, a sunroof or drop-top for easily surveying your "entertainment" equipment? The more expensive or trendy your make and model is, the heftier your get out of jail fine can be!

Note: These amenities give PoPo's an indication as to whether it's worth pulling you over, since their main objective is in reaching their quota for the month. But if asked, PoPo's will adamantly deny pulling you over because they have a BOLA (Babe On Lockdown Alert) quota to meet.

3. If you're a green/new *"I just got my license to roll!"* operator. PoPo's will immediately know you're inexperienced because you are either:

    a.) Stopping or accelerating too quickly.

    b.) Looking as if you're about to get *hit* on at any moment. This is better known as the Bambi Headlight Trance Syndrome.

    c.) Swerving to avoid no one in particular.

    d.) Ignoring all mandatory safety procedures while operating your vehicle.

You may have a legitimate license to roll, but you'll have no clue of what you are rolling up to!

4. If your state-of-being inspection stickers and tags have expired. This is a clear indication that you are operating your vehicle under the needy, lonely or desperate influence.

Note: PoPo's will also zero in on you when you've inadvertently or intentionally left your LED (Lonely, and Extremely Desperate) emergency distress flashers on.

5. The PoPo is in a forgiving mood. I.e., letting you go your merry way without further incident. In this case, you're released with a stern warning to not be pulled over by them again.

6. The PoPo is in an *unforgiving* mood and thereby decides to hold you to the laws of entrapment. If this happens and you are without sound self-counsel, you might be on your way to lockdown!

Any of the pervious scenarios may apply, and you may or may not be given a one-time warning or exemption. So, I must ask you, is it worth taking a chance like this? Do you feel *that* lucky?

You may perceive yourself as lucky or blessed to have 20/20 vision which will help when scanning for a PoPo up to 20 feet away. But you cannot rely solely on eyesight. Visual acuity can be deceptive. Remember, even you have fooled a few in your day!

By opting to rely on eyesight only, you will forgo the advantages of hindsight. In my opinion, hindsight is far superior to eyesight alone. Notice that I've dropped luck from the equation because we both know how that has worked so far.

Since luck is not reliable, you may be wondering why it's a mistake to lean too heavily on the ability to see? And doesn't seeing result in developing hindsight? Well, yes and no. If you are correctly interpreting what you are seeing, then hindsight is further developed. But more than likely,

Yvonne L. Jones

you will be attempting to quickly size up several different scenarios while also trying to navigate around probable speed traps. This will require very precise physical and mental work!

To accomplish this feat, you may be leaving yourself open to the whelms of luck, and *again* we all know how fleeting luck can be. It will also require you to somehow instantly activate super human vision, awareness, knowledge *and* the driving capabilities of Mario Andretti!

Even if you had all that going on, you'd still need some backup assistance. It's very easy to miss a cleverly concealed speed trap. Especially when your internal radar is not set up to function in the way it is meant to.

Your uniquely designed internal radar has several applications. But in this instance, it is an early warning alert for those human speed traps stationed at various junctions along your life route.

So, rest assured you *will* run into at least a couple of these speed traps in your lifetime. By now you may have this etched in your memory as I've reiterated this fact several times, but some of you have run into them repeatedly! And even though most of these run-ins will be for educational--enlightenment purposes only, would not shedding as little blood, sweat and tears as possible be a more desired outcome?

As you probably already know, a PoPo's speed trap is extremely proficient at initially concealing their incompatibility, selfishness, neediness, chronic negativity, abusiveness or even violence. You will not be able to avoid the trap simply because you will not see it, not until it's too late! If you have set your radar to only pick up surface stuff like looks, dress or things that may indicate a certain level of monetary accomplishment, then your radar will *not* alert you to those hidden speed traps you'd prefer to avoid.

It will also fail to scan for any of those endearing character traits you honestly desire to experience. Such as compatibility, understanding and the ability to express love and compassion--just to name a few.

Okay, I realize what I'm about to say next may not be received well, but here it is. One can only properly setup their internal radar to detect what they are deeply, consciously aware of. If surface stuff--window dressings are the things of higher priority to you in life or in seeking the One, then the following goes without saying. But you already know I'm about to say it.

Please don't attack the messenger, but more than likely *you* are exhibiting surface stuff as well and cannot in all honesty expect to cultivate a relationship any deeper than you are willing or capable of going. Correction. You can expect it, but it ain't gonna' happen!

Fair warning--you cannot set your radar to alert you to any potential ones who are fine, smart, confident, rich and beautiful, then be surprised or upset when they come with other stuff!

Here's some of the stuff I'm referring to. They're endowed with a huge out of proportion ego, not one ounce of common sense or true kindness, riches they intend to keep all to themselves, and beauty or genius they love promoting to *anyone* who will see and admire them as such.

I can't tell you how many times I've heard women say they want a rough-neck, ride or die guy who's not afraid to take risks, is exciting, thrilling and will love them to death. I know you see what's coming next, right? A month or two into the relationship, if that long, some of them will already be exhibiting battle scars.

We know all too well that some scars are physical. They

come in assorted colors, sizes and shapes like black, purple and swollen eyes, or missing teeth and broken bones. But a higher percentage of these battle scars are emotional--psychological.

There are several ways in which we can become scarred. Unfortunately, improper or inadequate guidance during ones early and influential years can sometimes set in motion an inclination to allow emotional, physical and psychological scars to develop.

Sometimes due to a dysfunctional relationship that occurred during childhood, some will unknowingly place themselves in harmful relationships in which continued scarring will be the norm.

There's the scarring related to losing one's individual power because their self-esteem has taken multiple hits, and subsequently been run into the dirt. Scars will also develop if one is driven to feel extreme anxiety and nervousness on a consistent basis. Or when attempting to avoid situations that resemble walking on razor-sharp, jagged egg shells.

They feel forced into taking such unorthodox, acrobatic steps because they have no idea what the "Thriller" might do to them next. They're antsy because they've come to believe that it's highly probable for them to somehow be loved to death!

Worst case scenario, some will tolerate this emotional or physical pain because they fear giving up too soon. The thinking is that at any moment their Thriller will have a sudden revelation and see what a wonderful gem of a person they have at their disposal.

However, the words *"have at their disposal"* takes on a dark, twisted meaning. In the eyes of these types of Thrillers, anyone willing to accept such cruel and unusual punishment is indeed disposable.

For those who have convinced themselves that waiting out the abuse is worth it, they give up more and more of their free will, awareness and power. When things get to this point, the alternative can seem even more terrifying for them.

Just imagine being left still longing for the One, the perceived better half of you that never comes. Then couple this unfulfilled longing with the fear of having to give up *any* expectations of *ever* experiencing genuine love and affection with the missing, and mistakenly regarded better half of you.

This type of perceived bleak and loveless destiny coupled with feelings of separation/loneliness or fragmentation/brokenness may seem far worse than any physical pain one can go through. It's sad to witness or to even imagine anyone enduring such an avoidable situation as this.

But just allow me to state for the record that I am by no means insinuating all roughneck, ride-or-die guys, operate in this way. As a matter of fact, I personally know of some who could loosely be categorized as roughnecks. They're usually very streetwise, not quite thugalicious, nowhere near gangster and would **never** treat the woman they proclaim to love or anyone non-threatening in a disrespectful way.

Yes, they can easily flip the script from Mr. Nice Guy to Mr. Terminator if anyone crosses the line or threatens to harm them or their love interest. But just as easily, they can be driven to tears, and I mean crying like a baby if anyone, including themselves does anything to hurt or deeply sadden the one they love.

It almost seems as if we enter a game of chance when seeking the One doesn't it? But there are some wonderful one's out there to connect with and yes, this includes you!

However, we don't often realize just how wonderful we truly are. We've been told a lot of erroneous things and because we take these things to heart, we will try just about every crazy scheme imaginable to make this one critical connection happen.

What's the result of all the madness we seem to go through when searching for the One? Sometimes seekers will get a hit that sticks. But for others, they're left dealing with the cleanup from a few soft messy hits that couldn't have possibly stuck around in the first place!

Sadly, if one ends up one-less too often, they may give up believing the one they desire exist at all. Or they will eventually lower their expectations well beyond their own recognition and accept anyone who comes along.

With several unsuccessful attempts to locate the One, many will fall prey to all types of lotions, potions, chants and gadgets, but especially the hype created by that ingenious Wizard we're all familiar with.

You know this Wizard by the magical, fantastical place it works its magic through, the Entertainment Industry. This industry often glorifies abusers, both male and female. It will endow them with fabulous exteriors while making excuses, exemptions or exceptions for their less than stellar interior.

What the Wizard of illusions is selling Joe and Jane Public are low quality goods at top dollar and realizing huge profits in return. It's unsettling to witness so many who are modeling their lives behind these fictitious, tantalizing images. Images that are being created at an astounding rate, and for the sole purpose of keeping the industry's (and its conglomerates) money train on track.

You see the industry has become adept at convincing its followers/fans to not only tune in again and again for the next mind numbing, mesmerizing curtain call, but to also emulate what they are seeing.

The industry is more than happy to sell Joe and Jane Public more flash and bang, more tricks and illusion for even more money, and will do so for as long as they can. Whether their tricks of the trade will have long or even short-term benefit for Joe and Jane Public is rarely factored into the equation.

Why do such dastardly things you ask? Think about it, why would they do otherwise? The Publics' (and just in case you're wondering, the Public's are us!) have already bought into the illusion, the lie--hook, line and sinker! The industry doesn't need to change anything to keep us, not when we're so willing *and* paying for the privilege mind you, to stay exactly where they want us to be.

So, what's the true price we pay for staying on board with such masters of illusion? We have become the poster children for what self-imposed, debilitating amnesia and memory loss does to a body. Too many of us no longer remember why we do what we do, who we truly are and what we're all about!

We have forgotten that we are much stronger and more beautifully made than any fancy outfits the Wizard can stitch *or* air brush together. The fact that we are regal and important *without* an emblem, or another's famous name covering our body parts is not even considered by most of us.

Ignoring or abandoning our true inheritance makes it easier to discard that which we are meant to embody as sovereign beings. Our brilliantly crafted crown of jewels, that of self-love and self-awareness has been set aside or pawned as mere trinkets.

In place of this priceless crown, we have attached

illusionary self-pride, dangerous self-ridicule, unawareness and occasionally synthetic or discarded human strands of hair! We are so much more than all the Wizard's emblems put together, and yet too often we feel the need to display these things as if they will make us better by doing so.

Now don't go getting your bloomers in a knot. I am not saying that the only way anyone can be authentic and happy is to remove, or get rid of their nice designer clothing, shoes, hairpieces, tats or whatever else they desire to wear.

What I am saying is this. No one should believe they need things, showpieces attached or added to themselves to feel complete or worthy, like someone of importance or someone who matters.

None of these outer things have ever had a part in creating who we are. Yet too many of us, from pre-teens to senior citizens whole-heartedly believe that if they are seen without these things, then they are by default deemed as lesser persons.

Maybe we should take into consideration what a showpiece does for us, aside from it possibly looking nice. Because remember, beauty is always in the eyes of the beholder. Sometimes the beholder is self but most times it's others.

Regardless of who is doing the beholding, the one thing a showpiece consistently does is to draw attention to *it*, while its wearer is under the false assumption of it drawing attention to them. Need proof of this? Here it is. I'm positive you've said or heard someone say the following statement many times before:

*"I love the outfit you're wearing! The color, style, cut and design are stunning! Where did you get **it**?"*

After making this statement, if you already know and care about the person displaying the showpiece; is interested in getting to know them, or if you're just being polite, *then* you'll acknowledge the one wearing the showpiece.

You may give them two thumbs up for looking fantastic while wearing such an awesome accessory. Or acknowledge them for being savvy enough to acquire such a great looking showpiece, even if it *doesn't* look so good on them! Here's the usual follow up statement:

"It really looks good on you!" Or *"It really complements the color of your hair, eyes and skin tone!"*

Did you get that? It is the showpiece that attracts the attention *first*. Then afterwards, whether genuinely or not, a compliment is extended to the one wearing it. This is a natural response or reaction when seeing something we either like or don't like. It doesn't necessarily mean we're being judgmental or accepting, envious or exaggerating.

Most of the time, it is just the expressing of one's personal preference for a thing. But too often the one on the receiving end of the compliment (or non-compliment) will take this type of interaction as personal, when in fact it has very little to do with them!

One's physical body also falls within the outer stuff category. Unless you're a highly attuned individual, the outer image--the holograph you see and pay attention to *first*, makes it's almost impossible to know without a doubt what an individual's authentic inner self will be.

We can't accurately gauge from a person's outer appearance their nature or disposition, or their gifts and talents. Nor will we know with certainty their passions, personal achievements, likes or dislikes.

The outer images we're initially captivated by rarely gives us a hint as to whether the individual is compassionate, creative, loving, caring or not. Even the individual exhibiting the showpiece may or may not associate their authenticity with the thing they are displaying.

Case in point. Let's say you walk into a store to make a purchase, and in walks what appears to be a biker from Hell's Kitchen--the seedier side of town. He's a big burly guy, sporting the traditional ZZ Top beard, black shades, jeans, leather jacket, and the brim of his cap is flipped to the back with a long-braided ponytail flowing from beneath it. Biker man is displaying quite a few showpieces, but the one that really gets your attention is what the black tee shirt he's wearing says:

"I Love A Hog Between My Legs!"

Beneath this declaration is the picture of a man driving a V-Rod Harley Davidson motorcycle with his beard and ponytail streaming behind him. It's all but apparent to you that *this* guy loves all things hog!

However, when he gets next to you in the checkout line, and you compliment him about the design and catchy phrase on his tee shirt, you discover that he is *not* what his holographic image displays.

"Oh...this? My son gave it to me as a joke. He thinks the biker looks a lot like me, which he does. But I'm a truck guy. The only bikes I've ever been on in my life are a tricycle and a 10 speed!"

Not only is he *not* a notorious biker in a gang, he's an ex-hippy turned sheep farmer who also loves raising honey bees and growing orchids as a hobby! Sort of lays to rest the theory of the dress, doesn't it?

Sometimes a dress, in this instance a Hell's Kitchen ensemble or any emblem, tool or title is just that. It is what it is and nothing more. Whether it has a special meaning or sentiment attached to it; it cannot tell us all that there is to know about the one exhibiting it.

For those of us who are not psychic, clairvoyant or

empaths, we're not privy to all if any of a person's unique life story through a mere glance! There must be the extending of an invitation, the willingness to share those formative elements of a person's life story.

However, that will not happen if either party is insecure or big headed; lacks confidence or humility, *or* see's themselves better or less than the other! No, that wasn't a rant. I was merely having a partial soap box moment.

When we stop growing or becoming more aware from the inside out and start believing we are less than capable of successfully navigating our own lives, we will eventually fall for just about anything.

What often follows the inner fall from self is the outer cover-up of self. If we believe we have fallen short in some way, we soon begin to feel overly exposed and that everyone can see all our perceived flaws and shortcomings.

At some point in life, each of us will experience these feelings to some degree. But no one wants to be viewed in this way, as less than others and to have everyone scrutinizing, pointing the finger and judging them.

So, to "save face" we usually make the more expedient decision to cover up. Covering up is quicker, is believed to look better and most definitely seems easier to do. The moment we decide to take this course of action, to hide by covering up, the Wizard's conveniently available eye-popping gadgets and accessories quickly come into play.

Do you feel weak and insignificant, or awkward and a wallflower? Then you will certainly feel much more confident and commanding inside of *their* specialized coverings. These coverings can be a car, clothing, jewelry, girl or boy toy, etc.

Apparently, these things have been designed to camouflage whatever doesn't measure up to socially acceptable standards. Hopefully, some of you have figured out that these standards have been set by those *within* the industry!

I'm assuming you don't believe for one second that you nor others are so demoralized that we'd set such impossible standards to be met and maintained. Or do you? Well, hopefully this will set your mind at ease. We did no such thing! *But* we have allowed demoralizing feelings to set in and here's why.

Now that we have become mesmerized, addicted to the Wizard's hypnotic eye candy, it is only fitting that we are provided further assistance. Since due to our addiction we cannot manage our lives on our own, it is the Wizard's task to help us feel better about the way we look, think and feel.

The Wizard is more than happy to convince us that the way we imagine we should appear, is a much better indicator of our greatness and eventual happiness. So, why would we even bother attempting to better know and understand ourselves and others? Unfortunately, we *are* addicts and prone to being irrational as well as irresponsible. Yeah, that was sarcasm.

But doesn't it seem to you that Wizards have modeled their script entirely from that of the dressmaker in the book, *The Emperor's New Clothes*. If you remember, the Emperor was *not* sporting the designer, noble wears the dressmaker had convinced him he was wearing. The Emperor was in fact stork naked and in more ways than one!

But just in case you don't remember the dressmaker or the naked Emperor, I'm sure you remember the Scarecrow in the Wizard of Oz. However, a fashionable wardrobe was of no interest to the Scarecrow, but he was in dire need of a brain.

He thought, believed, imagined (you *are* getting this...right?) that he didn't have one—a brain. And because of his missing appendage, he felt it made him appear less capable than others.

Yet, it was the Scarecrow who always came up with the most ingenious ideas! It was also the Scarecrow who masterminded the best actions to take as he and his motley crew journeyed to and through the sometimes deceptive, inhospitable Land of Oz.

What about the Lion who believed he lacked courage, and admitted he was even afraid of himself! That's something most of us would *never* have the courage to admit to anyone, let alone ourselves.

Though the Lion often felt afraid of his own shadow or to be more precise--his own tail, he proved to be courageous time and again. He did so even when performing a courageous deed exposed him to significant risk.

Then there was the Tin Man. He didn't think he had a heart, and yet he was the one who was more sensitive and empathetic to the feelings and concerns of his fellow sojourners. So much so, that he often became very emotional and cried until he became rusty! Which eventually rendered in-operable.

Each of them desired to receive the thing they believed was missing from their lives and willing or not, they faced many obstacles while in route to the Wizard. They didn't always feel they would reach their destination intact, but they somehow found enough courage to press on.

For some of us, present company included, one or two of the obstacles they faced would have sent us screaming and running away in the opposite direction! However, while being afraid, uncertain and mostly unprepared, they stayed the course.

It was not apparent to them at the time, but it was the facing of their fears which led to their character and strengths being greatly improved upon. During their journey, they demonstrated many times how courageous, smart, loving and compassionate they truly were. But *still* they needed confirmation from the Wizard!

Despite the impressive strides they each made, they remained unconvinced of any personal achievements being accomplished, and that what they *had* done didn't really amount to very much. Instead, they held the belief that only an all knowing, all powerful being such as the Wizard could grant them the internal, self-inspired qualities they each desired to have.

What happens next was totally unexpected by them. The motley crew discovers through a peek behind the curtains what should have been an immediate game changer! Through an unexpected peek into the Wizard's inner sanctum, they could see that he was in fact a small (both in statue *and* power) uncertain, lost and frustrated man who couldn't find his own way out of the predicament *he* was in.

Just as they were, he was stuck in a place or condition he didn't want to be in while having to masquerade as the all-powerful, all knowing Wizard. In other words, he was faking and shaking! This fake Wizard wanted something more meaningful for himself just as they did!

Though they could each see *and* hear with all six of their eyes and ears simultaneously, the Wizard's lack of vast knowledge and power, it was only *after* he'd bestowed upon them emblems, showpieces, objects of proclaimed authenticity, that they were finally willing to accept empowerment.

If that's not being under the spell of an illusion, I don't

know what is! Now, don't get all puffed up thinking you'd never fall for the same tricks they did. Their unawareness is typical of ours, even with all that some of us *think* we know currently!

For the Scarecrow who believed he didn't have a brain, a piece of paper in the form of a diploma granted him instant near genius IQ. He's able to quote mathematical theorem after receiving it. Really...a piece of paper did all that?

The Lion received the coveted Medal of Valor and as he pondered the word courage which was etched into the medal, he stood a bit straighter and seemed to be filled with Rambo-like courage and tenacity. But he was already Ramboish *before* he'd ever met the Wizard or received the medal!

Next it was the Tin Man's turn to receive his empowerment. He was given a heart-shaped watch. As he listened to the steady, symbolic sound the ticking heart made, he was immediately flooded with emotion, with all the loving feelings his mechanical heart implied he now possessed. But how was he able to be so loving, sensitive and caring prior to receiving it?

Wizards love creating tons of alluring coverings for our continued distraction. However, there's no permanence in the things they produce and promote. Their garments and gadgets always seem to fall in and out of season at just the right time. Then lo and behold and at more than the appropriate cost, a newer more improved covering is made available.

In our zeal for the best cover-ups, wizards will insist we utilize these things *if* we are to experience all that we desire to. As you may be able to tell, it's difficult for me to imagine anyone intentionally choosing to remain uncomfortable in their own skin. Or that one would rather be unaware of how to activate and then take full advantage of their inborn greatness.

Of course, we have free will and can do whatever we choose whether it benefits us or not. But I think we often put off doing the required inner work because we believe it's just too difficult and time consuming. Or maybe it's because we sometimes see ourselves under the unfavorable glare cast by that murky, dismal, green-tinted light associated with failure.

The color of light I'm referring to is much like the color of the Wicked Witch of the West. Who by the way, no one in Oz wanted to associate with. Sure, she wasn't the most likable or agreeable person to be around, but her disagreeable disposition didn't have the power to sway everyone's love for the various shades of green.

Remember, except for the Witch, everyone else were happy residents of the Emerald City. But as you already know, most don't care to be ostracized like the Witch. To avoid this hurtful form of segregation, some will take whatever steps they deem necessary.

I'm guessing you're wondering exactly where will these steps lead them to? It's believed these steps will lead them to that highly coveted, inclusive, member's only stamp of approval one seeks from others. Some are determined, bewitched to gain the approval from those who are endowed with the more fashionable, alabaster golden-tinted glow of success.

For those who believe they must radiate glowing success, there are no limits as to how far they will go to be seen and coveted in this way. No drab, murky green, unappealing tint for this bunch!

So, what are the benefits of all the exclusive inclusiveness they seek? Not nearly what one would imagine. Far too often the only thing they receive is a fleeting, insincere acknowledgement of a thing they already possess. Oh, and more debt!

Are you asking yourself if it's more productive to invest your time, focus and money on things that will greatly benefit others, aka Wizards, when you will not even consider doing those beneficial things for yourself? Do you ever wonder if it is more expedient to simply fall in line with another's standard of success as opposed to considering your own?

If you're not asking yourself these questions, then consider the following. Ignoring or attempting to cover up how you really feel, trading down or giving up on the things you truly desire to experience in life, is a strong indicator that your internal radar tracking device is *not* uniquely calibrated.

If you're determined to hook up with the One or anything else you desire in life, then you'll have to do a bit of in-house tinkering to recalibrate it. There's just no getting around that. However, it's not a monumental task to accomplish, as there is no huge learning curve you must master.

Yes, you'll have to incorporate a new way of thinking, and learn to respond differently to the valuable life lessons coming your way. With empowered thinking, you'll begin to realize that deescalating the many faces of fear is not half as difficult as you've been led to believe.

For example, facing eventualities and rising to any challenge is more beneficial *and* rewarding then faking enlightenment and running away! The first action empowers you for an increase, the second one does not.

Admit it, you are already aware that there are some things you're currently doing that are not the least bit beneficial. You also know that there are other things which would be beneficial if you'd simply take the necessary action at the right time.

When you get honest with yourself and choose to empower rather than belittle or dismiss your desired intentions as impossible to attain, then some of your recalibration process will come naturally. The rest can be learned. Hopefully, you'll come to a better understanding of a few things.

One, that you already have access to an inspired, inner component capable of unlimited awareness--just as the Scarecrow demonstrated. Two, that you can be a courageous lion or lioness regardless of your fears. Third but not least--it's possible to be more loving and compassionate with yourself and others *without* doubting, feeling overwhelmed, getting rusty and unable to move forward like the Tin Man.

All it takes is the willingness to make a few adjustments. And most definitely, after you've fine-tuned your radar to specs, you'll have to turn *and* keep it on. Then it can better assist you!

CHAPTER 4

Love and Happiness, Fear and Pain

Prior to you becoming the mirror image of the One you seek, you may have come from a place of neediness, desperation, loneliness and fear. Maybe you once accepted and took to heart the following fear-based statements:

"Having a piece of a man or woman is better than having no man or woman at all! No pain, no gain! It's cheaper to keep them! If you don't grab them, somebody else will!"

But now you know better. You don't need someone to pull you together, to prop you up or to fix you. You know better because you are not a bunch of fragmented body parts or brain cells held together by a few flimsy pieces of tape!

I do realize that sometimes it feels like you're falling apart or unraveling at the seams, but you don't need someone else's masking tape or super glue to hold you together. You're whole and complete all by yourself! No chemical adhesives are ever required.

And because of your new, ever evolving self-awareness, you are no longer in the business of trying to piece together another individual either! Remember, no one can do that for another. True "peace" work is only done by the individual who holds the intention of mending themselves. Without the inclination to do so, inner peace and wholeness will never happen.

Neither should anyone believe that with love sometimes there's pain--as if pain is a by-product of love! But this cannot be because love is the opposite of pain or fear. Love does not hurt or harm.

However, feelings of unworthiness, dread, hopelessness, constant doubts and anxieties, trepidation and many more of the fear-based feelings we too often experience does hurt *and* produces harm.

By now, you're beginning to understand that it is your own unique heart-mind connection you must get comfortable with and further develop. Feeling *and* knowing that you are whole despite outer appearances or circumstances is vital to your continued growth, awareness and happiness.

As a matter of fact, this inner knowing of self will be what attracts the perfect One to you. Or alert you when you're contemplating jumping the gun and getting into a relationship you should holster for the time being.

Yes, that was a Texas inspired analogy. However, when you are within the initial stages of coming into your wholeness, you will need a few reminders or some nourishing foods for thought.

You can think of this nourishment as vital sustenance which will empower and assist you when engaging probable ones and bypassing PoPo's. As a matter of fact, it's always best to have a form of sustainable energy no matter what it is you desire to accomplish in life!

I call these nourishing energy bites my little golden love nuggets. Keep in mind, they are suggested daily allowances only and not nourishment guidelines written in stone. If these love nuggets don't seem appetizing enough for you to digest, then simply go with your gut, with what feels like the most natural, uncompromising, stress-free thing for you to consume!

Although people are similar in many ways, we do have different nourishment requirements at various times in our lives. No one food will completely nourish, support or be pleasing to everyone. Never consume or do what does not feel right for you.

You know how people can be. We love giving unsolicited advice or forcing our opinions on others. But and you may already know what I'm about to say next, just allow them to do that, because short of you removing yourself from their presence, you really can't stop them!

However, it doesn't mean you must adhere to anything they suggest, advise or have an opinion about. As a matter of fact, you can counter their opinion about you with your own! They just might surprise you by liking yours more than theirs. Even if they don't think your opinion is worth a two-week-old biscuit, never fall for the doubt and fear lures they'll eventually cast your way.

They may insist that a potential one is trust worthy even though you sense they are not. Or that a certain situation is nothing to be overly concerned about when in fact you should be. Example:

"Well, they have an excellent job! So, what if they're thirty-years old and have never moved out of their momma's house! You better grab that up while you can. If you don't, someone else will!"

My counter to this fear lure is that you allow someone else to have at them! Until you learn why an outwardly capable adult continues living with their mother, you should be leery of grabbing up this catch or anyone close to them.

He or she may very well be a mama's or daddy's baby

with no intentions of leaving them until death do they part! *Or* they could be a very loving child who's attending to their chronically ill parent but understands that they are no longer literally attached by the umbilical cord.

Maybe they're the only child, and they want to make sure their parent(s) are appropriately looked after and that their life will be as comfortable as they can make it. But until you know which mind-set rules them, refuse to go along with any hasty instructions grounded in fear or desperation.

If you do not ignore these lures/traps, you will be committing yourself to a course of action you're not truly ready for. Think about it. If you *were* ready, there'd be no temptation needed to lure you into action.

On the contrary, when you are ready to bust a move, it will feel like the most natural next step to take. No one is truly ready for a situation in which they have been pushed, tricked or lured into. Even when all the tempting has been self-generated!

What happens when a person succumbs to someone else's or their own fear tactics? That's an easy one to answer because it is a common occurrence that has been well documented.

Those who easily succumb to fear almost always obsess about not being able to hold onto the very one or thing they desired to acquire. Their fear seems to easily escalate.

For them, it is imperative to hold onto that which they believe is needed to live a happy life. And because of their obsessive compulsiveness, they will undertake one desperate or dangerous action after another.

Sometimes their actions can become like those of a hoarder. Hoarding is the compulsion for one to stock pile things. They fear letting go of certain items because there may come a time when they'll need all 500 of them!

The things they hoard can range from something as simple and easy to acquire as paper cups. Or they'll obsess over something more complicated to hold onto and harder to maintain, like people.

Yes, a person can hoard other people they desire to be in relationship with. You've heard of them before or may know of one personally. They are the ones who have several friends with benefits on reserve. They're better known as players and their obsessions are known as side pieces.

Much like hoarders, players never want to be without whatever it is they believe maintains the feelings they must have. Maybe there's the need for companionship to ward off loneliness, for adoration to stoke the ego, sex to validate their ability to feel, or control to prove they have mastery over others.

Whatever the need is, they will juggle people to ensure that it is met. Some will confess to genuinely caring about every one of their friends, while others will make it known that they could care less about them.

Should one friend drop out, they're not overly concerned as there are several backups in their holding cue. However, if they get a little nervous about the number of reinforcements available to them, they will simply do what any bona fide hoarder would--grab more replacements just in case!

I'm sure at this point in your life, you already know how fear operates. Fear breeds more fear and tarnishes everything you think about touching. Lingering too long within a fearful train of thought only insures greater fears will develop. If left unchecked, fear multiplies like an aggressive strain of virus invading and taking over your will to think outside of it.

Initially, harmless appearing doubts will seem to have a personality like that of a trustworthy advisor, an advisor who genuinely cares for you and doesn't want to see you in pain or headed for trouble.

But in no time at all, your once helpful advocate will morph into the advisor from Hell! One who is *always* in your ear and has complete confidence in telling you…no, *insisting* that you are not doing enough!

If you continue listening to this bogus advisor, it will have you believing you're losing out on something or everything, that you're running out of time, you're undeniably unworthy or useless *and* on the brink of being replaced!

When you elect to get into an arm-wrestling match with fear's flawed advice, know that the odds are already stacked against you. You will more than likely lose. And is this really the way you want to begin a life of co-creation with another, in a constant tug of war with fear?

Yes, we each have our own personal bouts with fear. Sometimes they're out-right slugfests in which we win, tie or lose a few. But do we have to allow fear to dictate our every action or thought? Do we even have to fight with fear?

No, I don't think we do. There's always the option to choose the quiet, gentle persuasive power of love and happiness instead of the unsubstantiated, overbearing loudness of fear and pain.

Unfortunately, we are in the habit of listening to big mouth scaredy cat fear and following its lead. We rush blindly ahead and by default, we also rush to feel the pain that follows. Sure enough, we end up with *someone* but not the *best* one for us. Afterwards, we're devastated because we realize we could have waited, taken more time and thereby avoided all the pain that follows the fear of losing out.

Seems ironic, doesn't it? The things we fear the most, the things we try the hardest to avoid are the very things we end up experiencing. However, it really isn't ironic at all. It's simply the Focus Factor at work.

Whatever we spend a great deal of focused attention on and highly charged emotions or feelings with, we manifest and thereby experience. Whether it is love and happiness or fear and pain. The things we experience are *not* coincidence.

Nor do things happen to us because we're having a run of good or bad luck. Our life experiences are not brought about by the possession of lucky talismans, the breaking of mirrors or by walking on or over cracks in a sidewalk.

Neither are the things we manifest (experience or create) is due to outer manipulations like those of a magician's sleight-of-hand tricks or illusions. We experience things in life because of how and what we focus on.

However, do not confuse focused attention with pure, untainted intention. Awareness is what distinguishes one from the other. Your degree of emotional *and* mental focus makes it possible for you to receive what you clearly and steadfastly desire to experience, *or* what you fear, dread and stress about experiencing.

As you can see, it doesn't matter if what you're focusing on is truly desired or greatly dreaded. Whichever one you resonate more deeply and often with; will be the experience you pull into your life.

For example, you may have the best intentions of connecting with that special One. You've done a lot of the inner work and you already know what you desire to experience within a relationship. *But* despite your very best intentions of connecting with the One, you more often worry about how difficult or near impossible it will be to find them.

You begin focusing more on all the things that could slow down or stop this meeting from ever occurring. I'm sure you agree that this is the wrong way to focus on anything you desire to experience!

This type of back-door, chronic worrying nullifies even the best of intentions, and subsequently brings to you the things you fear and worry about the most. Other than providing a clear indication that you're focusing on the wrong things, jumping on the fear train is not productive at all. Yet, we do this to ourselves quite often.

When you utilize pure intention to realize the thing you desire, there's no more guessing, back-tracking, re-thinking, disbelieving doubts or fears connected with it. With pure intent, what you desire stands strong *and* attainable no matter how long it takes!

As a matter of fact, time will cease to be relevant, because you'll instinctively know that your desires will show up at the best possible moment! You know, there's a very good reason we are told by consciously aware masters *not* to fear or worry.

Yes, I know! Being free of fear/worry seems like an impossible state of being to maintain. Because in our minds there's always some situation or someone eager to push all our worry buttons. Well, you are right to believe that, because *you* are always that someone who's pushing the buttons!

However, since concerns or worries will pop up every now and then, the best way to counteract them is to learn how to recognize a fear-worry train when it pulls into your station. In this way, you'll know to let that train roll right on past you!

But if you get distracted for a moment and somehow end up boarding a worry train, you can disembark quickly. Pressing the emergency stop button gets you off that impending train wreck and back on the right track!

"How" you ask? It's as simple as saying the following:

"No, I'm not going any place full of worry and fear. Why on Earth would I want to subject myself to that pain? As a matter of fact, I'm not going there today or tomorrow. There's a better place for me, one full of empowerment, inspiration and all the things I can desire to experience. I'm going there!"

Say it *and* mean it! You will be surprised and amazed at how empowered you'll feel by saying these simple words of affirmation! Go ahead, try it right now and see how you feel.

Eventually, you will become keenly aware of how an approaching worry train feels and sounds. You'll also recognize where it's trying to take you. Then you'll instinctively know when to switch tracks so that impending train wreck is moving in the opposite direction of your intended destination!

In this book, my intention is to demystify those menacing relationship train wrecks so many of us worry about. However, in the book, *How To Strengthen Your Gut, Lose The "But" And Live Your Life Regret Free,* I go into much greater detail about how and why you should stop being fearful and worrying so much.

Now, I'll just to take a stab at what some of you might be thinking, that sometimes you experience things through no fault of your own. But whether you see it as yours or someone else's fault, you're the one being affected by it and you will have to be the one to resolve the issue.

Fault finding does two things and neither is productive.

For one, it hinders you from recognizing the *real* issue. Two, it makes it almost impossible to take corrective steps, so the issue is resolved, and you can move on stronger and wiser than you were before.

Please don't make it someone else's responsibility to change the way you think or feel. As much as you may love to pass that responsibility on to another, I believe you already have a sneaking suspicion that thinking and feeling is an inside job only! At least by now I hope you do. However, at times some tend to believe that how they think, or feel is a direct result of the influence or actions of others.

"He did all the things to make me love him! Then he made me hate him when he cheated on me!"

As devastating as this type of situation can feel for the one on the receiving end of this type of betrayal, no one can implant a feeling into another. We choose to love or hate whether there be little or extreme reasons for doing so.

In fact, when we attempt to relinquish control over our thoughts and feelings, we do ourselves a great disservice, and *attempt* to give others far too much power over us. We willingly consent to disempower ourselves when we respond in this way.

For anyone past the age of puberty and surely those with a few decades of life experiences under their belt, they've already made decisions about the things they like, don't like or may possibly like in the future.

When others interact with you, they're just reminding or helping you to re-establish, re-enforce or reconsider your preferences, your likes, dislikes and probabilities. They may not be aware that they're doing this, but you should! From the initial point of interaction with others, when and how you respond is entirely up to you. You may decide to roll around in the loving thoughts or feelings they have reactivated for you and enjoy every single moment of it.

Or you'll come to a screeching halt and put to an abrupt end whatever it is you do not desire to continue experiencing with them. Yes, it really is that simple and yes, it can also get confusing at times. But again, the confusion only comes about because we have a knack for complicating things.

I believe we are born with the instinct to establish and support certain needs and wants. That's how we survive *and* thrive. Yet some whom we interact with believe that at certain times, attending to one's personal needs and wants is not acceptable. That it is in fact being selfish or inconsiderate.

If this is the opinion of a loved one, it usually creates a dilemma for the one being accused of selfishness. On one hand, we want to do what's best for self. On the other hand, we may also want to please or do what's best for others.

Sometimes we can work it out and everyone's happy. Then there are times when we cannot find that happy balance and feathers will surely be ruffled! Each is upset and each one accuses or blames the other.

But who gets to manage, adjust, ignore, enjoy, dislike or love what is thought or felt if *not* the individual doing the thinking and the feeling? Wouldn't it be better to find *your* happy medium first, since no one can do that for you?

Then after you've balanced yourself, be it your emotions, thoughts, expectations or reactions, you'll be more willing and capable of managing for others what you can, while allowing them to do the same. I don't know, maybe I'm selfishly biased, but for me it sounds like the perfect plan for all parties concerned!

Remember, no matter how hard others try to convince you or how often they attempt to slap you with a guilt subpoena, you are *not* responsible for their feelings, thoughts, likes or dislikes. These are things each of us have already established or should. But just so you know, *you* will always be responsible for yours!

Now, are you ready to fine tune that radar of yours? I hope so, because that's what you're doing in the next chapter! Since you've made it this far, I'm believing you've gathered some information that can be useful in your life. So why not take a few more steps and position yourself to crossing the finish line with ease?

Did I mention that fine tuning your radar doesn't hurt? As a matter of fact, this type of adjustment will feel much better than those others' you've become accustomed to making. Remember the last PoPo you had to painfully detach yourself from? Well, this process will be several steps gentler then that one. I promise!

CHAPTER 5

Avoiding Mr. or Miss PoPo

You already know you must recalibrate your internal radar tracking device to avoid PoPo's and to align yourself with that desired one. But most are completely unaware of how to do this.

Many have functioned for so long with theirs being calibrated incorrectly, until they don't know where to begin adjusting. I so dislike sounding like a broken record, but adjustments are very simple to make. Elevate yourself by starting from the top, with what you truly desire to experience the most.

This is the time for you to be self-centered and to go bold! Begin with the things you desire to find in that lovely one and go from there. Decide the most beneficial character traits you have no intention of compromising with.

Place them from highest to lowest priority. In this way, you can avoid being mesmerized by the fancy bling-bling cart your steed or mare may be dragging around as an attention getter only.

You will thank yourself later when this saves you from feeling regrets because you've hitched your wagon to the

Yvonne L. Jones

proverbial horse of an unusual color. A horse who by the way is *not* in route to Lover's Meadow but to the glue factory! In that type of environmental wasteland, there will be very little present enjoyment and no future pleasure for *you* with them while there!

So, what is it you desire most, that they be courageous and fearless as opposed to timid or reckless? How about kind and gentle and not mean-tempered, pushy *or* a push over?

Are you envisioning the One as capable of expressing their inner most feelings, thoughts, dreams and goals? Or will you be content with guessing, with pulling that information out of them if they're secretive, or dismissive when it comes to expressing such things?

Will you appreciate them being a leader who will also follow or them being a follower who never leads? Is your preference for the one who is health conscious and avoids known determents to their total wellbeing? Or will you be comfortable with them occasionally or heavily smoking, drinking, over eating, taking drugs or engaging in other risky activities?

Don't be afraid to ask for what you want because if *you* don't ask for it, who will? After receiving the thing you've asked for, if it later becomes unimportant then no harm, no foul.

The same applies to those character and physical traits you do *not* desire to find in your beautiful one. Try not to get into the habit of making exceptions and coming up with excuses as to why you should downsize or make a trade-off simply to gain other quality traits you see in them.

Let's just imagine that they are fun, sweet, loving and generous, and you love all these qualities *but* they're also into recreational drug use. Every time you see them, they're smoking something, popping pills or guzzling gin! However, *you* are adamantly against taking drugs of any kind.

In this instance, now is not the time for you to waffle or bend over backwards. Stand your ground and hold out for the one you truly desire because they are out there waiting for you to make up your mind!

Second, and this is the visually fun part, list the physical traits you're seeking in your sensual other half. Follow the exact same method used in identifying character traits you desire. Be completely honest with both the character and physical traits you are looking for.

If there is a must have trait you want to see in them, then expect to find it in your One! Don't compromise or become doubtful about what you truly desire to experience. As a matter of fact, this is the perfect time to follow the recommendations of that once popular fast food slogan. *"Have it your way!"*

Are you more comfortable with the one being a casual, eclectic, conservative or trendy dresser? How about hair? Should the man for you have facial and head hair, either or none? Will you be okay with the one being short, tall, slim, of average build, a bit thicker or with popping pecs?

Apply the same process for pinpointing the physical traits you'd love to find in the woman you desire to be with. But just remember anything written in stone can be chiseled over.

It's possible that while you're in the self-growth and discovery mode, your preferences can and more than likely will change. This is exactly the reason you shouldn't rush this process. Instead you should grow until you know!

You may come to realize that some of things you were demanding your beautiful one should have, were traits *others* may have suggested or considered as important for those seeking the One.

However, because of your deeper understanding and awareness, some of the attributes you were seeking before now seem petty or have become a non-issue. You're no longer the same unaware individual who simply goes along with the crowd and follows any ole leader.

The main purpose and premise of this book is to help stimulate and cultivate the realization that *you* are the best leader of your life! It's the reason you have the free will to act at all. Which means you can and should follow *your* intuition, *your* heart, *your* good feelings and *your* own mind concerning what is best for you.

Now is the time for you to stop mindlessly incorporating others questionable beliefs, ideals or principles. Especially when those concepts place everyone or thing into one overly crowded little box. Though similar in many ways we, *you* are not like everyone else. You are you!

Your life experiences, your level of awareness, your talents and desires guarantee you are unlike any other individual on the planet! If you really think about it, the only thing that makes us similar is that we are all this way. Alike in some ways and totally different in others. Mind blowing, isn't it?

Here's the third and last step to recalibrating your internal radar, and this too is quite simple. Review the requirements on your *"I've got to have this!"* and *"I'm not even going there!"* lists, then check to see if *you* meet those qualifications as well.

Of course, I'm referring more to character traits than to physical ones because if you're a male seeking a female, you will not be expected to have 38D breasts or curvy hips. However, if one of your requirements is that they are fit and healthy then *you* should at least be that. Lay all your cards on the table; be completely honest about how you measure up against your own list.

If you're close to those requirements, then you'll only need to make a few minor adjustments. If you are at or above those requirements, then you're good to go! Your internal radar is now fine-tuned and you're ready to engage with the One.

But, if you are nowhere near several of your requirements then...come on now, let's get real. How does one even fix their lips to form the words to ask for something they are not willing to give or to exemplify?

Okay, I'm speaking hypothetically now because this may or may not apply to you. But if you desire the One to be kind, honest and giving and *you* are mean-tempered, dishonest and selfish, then you have some serious soul searching *and* self-work to do. Recalibrating might take a bit longer.

On the other end of the spectrum, if you're okay with the one being healthy but not as fine as Adonis, then it's perfectly okay that *you're* healthy but not as fine as Aphrodite. Are you seeing how this works?

YOU must first mirror, become the One you are seeking. Once you begin exhibiting all the endearing traits and characteristics you desire to see in *them*, then you will never have to concern yourself with being stalked by Mr. or Miss PoPo!

Sure, a few will approach you because you will be radiating so much confidence, poise and powerful grace until their curiosity will get the better of them. But they will quickly realize you have somehow peeped their undercover PoPo facade, and that you've done so *without* having to deal with any of their drama or shenanigans!

Yvonne L. Jones

It will be obvious to them that you are aware, more than comfortable with who you are, that you know exactly what you want and how to go about getting it. Right off the bat, it will be apparent that you will *not* entertain any of their games, period. You're coming from a different place, a place they are unfamiliar with, and probably unwilling to tread upon. This leaves them with no other option *except* to move around!

Isn't this a wonderful thing to happen? That they simply drop off without any physical prodding or inappropriate language on your part? You bet it is! With their timely and much desired exit, you are free to engage with more potential ones. That's great news! That's, *"Do a little ditty and let the good times roll"* news!

Of course, you will be saving the last dance for that special one but there's no reason why you can't celebrate your completeness now. Remember, you are whole and complete all by yourself. Others can only add to your completeness, somewhat like a bonus or gift. However, if the bonus or gift is lost, taken away or no longer desired, you are still able to function because you're already complete!

Now, this doesn't mean you should walk around proclaiming from the mountain tops that you don't need anybody in your life. That would be foolish and a lie. We need one another. Without others to interact with, we'd experience a lonely, regretful and painful life.

However, I'm sure you've had the pleasure of interacting with a few individuals who were so disagreeable until it was impossible to engage with them on a continuous basis. Given enough time, their actions will alienate just about anyone. From the mild tempered and reasonable individual to the most dynamic, powerful and assertive one, neither can last very long with the antics of a PoPo!

Popo's seem to have an affinity for saying or doing the most inappropriate things at the best and worst of times. And the bewildering thing is, they don't seem to have a clue that it is *their* actions pushing others away.

When you encounter people pushers like this, you *know* their radar if off--way off! So, I'll just caution you right now. Do Not attempt to fix them, to tell them what their problem is, or suggest why no one likes being around them. As sincere as you may be to help them "see the light" you will regret it!

I have seen people get into heated altercations, some would even escalate to physical violence and all because one tried to help "fix" or set straight the other. No one likes to be told they need fixing, even when it's apparent to others that they *do* need to make some adjustments in their life.

If you fall for the grandiose allure of being the designated fixer-upper of people, you will be inviting certain types of PoPo's into your life, guaranteed! And an open invitation to a PoPo is never a good thing. What types of PoPo's would that be, you ask? For starters:

Type 1 PoPo: The *"I know everything about everything and I will prove it to you!"* type. Need I explain more?

Type 2 PoPo: This type will start an argument just to get and hopefully keep you engaged. It's their odd way of interacting with others.

Type 3 PoPo: Type three will only address all the things they perceive *you* need help with fixing, since they have no issues whatsoever. They will enlighten you as to the exact moment *you* broke, what caused you to break and why you might be better off remaining that way. See, I told you! You don't want to go there with them.

Type 4 PoPo: This is the type who appears to agree with you: *"You're right, but I don't know what to do about it. You seem to have a better grasp of this issue than I do. Maybe you can help me work through it…if you don't mind?"*

Note: Bear in mind that this type 4 PoPo's statement requires more clarification as it is spoken in code. Here is the translation:

*"Will you give me all of your time so that you can show me everything I need to know? Can you hold my hand, counsel me morning, noon and night for years on end and before I ever think about getting it, **or** until you drop your guard against allowing me full access to your mind, body and soul?"*

Type 5 PoPo: I'm sure you've accidently bumped into one of these types before. They are the loud, boisterous, verbally repetitive know it all's. This type will proclaim all things with lively animation, resonating volume and unlimited replays. You are bound to be driven mad if you get and stay cornered by this type.

Type 6 PoPo: I have labeled type 6 the Atomic PoPo, and for good reason. This type is the fusion of all the others with an additional twist. Atomic PoPo's are all knowing, argumentative, impeccable and above reproach, conniving, loudly obnoxious and not afraid to use military style psychological or physical tactics to get what they want.

Now, I'll leave it up to you to decide if any of these types is 100 percent unaware as to how they adversely affect others. Since I tend to be a realist and an optimist, I believe sometimes they have a clue. They know. But for all those other times, they apparently lose all clues and every hint associated with one!

Whatever you believe their true intentions to be, you do not want to deeply entangle yourself with individuals at this level of consciousness. Again, I've seen others who have tried and the only thing they achieved was unnecessary pain and suffering. Trust me, you do not want to go there with any of them.

However, I realize you are the decision maker, the leader of your life. You get to decide whether you'll attempt to crack that nut or not! And no, I am not calling PoPo's nut jobs. That would be rude. I'm merely expressing the difficulties you will meet when attempting to help them, because they have no intentions of helping *you* to enlighten them! Remember, in their eyes, they're just fine.

And don't worry, I will not be the one who after the fact, throws it in your face that I warned you against attempting such a risky endeavor. So, I'm telling you now, Don't Do It! Avoid even responding to their sly request for a tinny-tiny bit of more interaction. Turn around immediately and walk away as fast as you can. Run if you must. After you've made it to a safe place, you can thank me then.

I know, I'm being comical but I'm also serious. Remember, you're no longer in the fixer-upper business. That's not your job in life. Thankfully they have trained professionals who attempt to perform this hazardous job.

I say they attempt to because as you already know, no one can fix another individual. The only thing anyone can really do is to shine a light on whatever the other's issue appears to be, and hopefully prod them in the direction of a deeper inner connection and awareness. If they're inclined to listen, then they will adjust themselves.

But even if a PoPo somehow falls through the cracks and those professionals can't or won't perform this desperately needed duty, what do you think your chances are at being successful with it? Especially if *you* are still in the process of awakening to certain levels of self-awareness.

If you haven't become aware or intuitive enough to discern whether your actions will help or hurt others *and* yourself, then do nothing. Neither should you rush into action if you're coming from a state of over confidence, criticism or frustration.

No one benefits when the "helper" is coming from any one of those ego-based states of being. I know, suppressing the urge to help anyone in such dire need of emotional support may seem like the opposite of love and compassion. But in this instance, it is not.

Allowing people to be who they are even when what they do is detrimental to themselves, demonstrates your love and compassion for their free will to make any life choices they deem appropriate. You don't have to agree with the choices they're making, but you must agree that it is their choice to make!

Do you know someone with an addiction? Their dependency can be to prescription drugs, alcohol, food, sex, shopping or the next exciting thrill. If what they are doing is not illegal and doesn't pose an imminent danger to themselves, others or property, there is nothing you or anyone else can do about it.

Sure, you can rant and rave, set up a surprise intervention or employ gentle persuasion to get them to seek help. Whatever efforts you employ, it is entirely up to them to listen and then agree with what you or anyone else believes is best for them.

Even if your argument is in line with what family, ex-addicts and doctors have already told them concerning how their addiction is slowly or quickly harming or killing them, they alone hold the option to ignore or accept any advice given.

So, if you are unlike those few masters who could heal or change people with a touch, a glance, a smile or words that could shatter the most resistant mind and heart, just bow out with as much grace as you can muster! No one can hold it against you.

Here's something that will help you to avoid falling into the trap of fixing a PoPo or anyone else who falls outside of the PoPo category. It is a powerful affirmation statement of co-creative alignment with self and the One:

"I do not need another to complete me or to compete against me. They need not overly concern themselves with how to make me feel, see or be a better one. I am already capable of adding to my individual growth and awareness.

What I desire is that my partner in co-creation compliment and add to the experiences we each desire to have. I'm in excited anticipation of creating with one who is just as excited and in tune with their growing awareness, individual wholeness and universal oneness.

This partner will understand that co-creation is the act and the art of giving and receiving that which is beneficial to both. That there is nothing greater than the love, fun, adventure and appreciation for those moments we each desire to share.

How can we not grow with all of this to inspire us upward and onward? I'm seeking that co-creator who resonates with me in the now and the next now to come if we desire to do so. How wonderful will these experiences be!

This is the one I'm in alignment for and I will not have to ask,

"Are you the One?" It will be evident the moment I experience the wholeness of them, and I will allow us to be. We will be as One."

CHAPTER 6

The 60 Second Countdown

Here it is, the 60 second countdown! Don't worry, this countdown is not something that will back fire or explode on you if you don't get through it before the timer goes off. There is no actual timer. You can slow, speed read, pause, back up or contemplate however long you need to. Get through this process at your own pace. Remember, this is all about you!

The 60 Second Countdown title is not meant to be taken literally but metaphorically. It's simply a linear way of applying a few techniques that will help keep you focused on what's most important to you. The big picture! Naturally, this picture includes the One being in that snapshot with you!

Since you've made it this far in the book, I'm not going to *assume* you want to experience the best life can offer. I'm certain that you do. Why else would you put up with me for this long if you didn't? Morbid curiosity?

I'm giving you kudos for loving yourself enough to grow. I know it's not always easy to get real with yourself *about* yourself. Sometimes it takes a lot of courage *and* strength to tear down those unreliable or no longer desired parts of yourself.

You better understand that we are sometimes creatures performing oblivious unproductive habits. Some tend to do the most unbeneficial things over and over again without ever taking note as to why they are repeatedly performing unproductive or harmful acts.

Even when it's fully understood that one shouldn't be doing what they're doing, they will continue to do it anyway! Yes, this boggles the most logical minds and yet these types of disempowering actions are performed with apparent ease.

Therefore, a bit of demolition and cleanup work is in order. Tearing down and then removing all the debris left over from those harmful, success blocking habits makes it possible to begin building up a more solid, stable you. But no one goes through this renovation process alone.

The things I've learned and will continue to learn about loving the life I intend to live, are not insights I've acquired all by my lonesome. It has taken every single individual and situation I've had the pleasure and pain of experiencing, to nudge or push me to the place I am today.

I'm wishing that whole and happy place for you as well. But understand this, you will not arrive at that place of contentment if you are still mourning uncomfortable or painful past experiences. You'll have to find a way to dismantle those too. Better yet, why not celebrate them!

Why on Earth would you celebrate something that was once so painful for you? Well for one, those uncomfortable or painful experiences captured your undivided attention, didn't they? They caused you to pause and to take note, even if just for a moment.

Not only that, they were instrumental in helping you to realize what you do and do not want to experience in your life. They made it apparent that adjustments were needed *if* you desired a different outcome outside of pain. That's why.

Those not so pleasant experiences can become your greatest allies and most valuable life lessons. Remember the lessons and leave all the other disempowering stuff where it belongs, behind you!

I'm sure during the time you were going through the rough part of your wilderness training, you were often consumed with a burning desire to back-slap into the next century *whoever* you felt was responsible for hurting you.

It's a good thing you must release all the gory details concerning who did what to you and why, or when and how they did it. If you don't, *they* will forever be the villain who is victorious over you, and *you* will always be the victim who never receives enough validation to move forward and beyond the experience.

This is the reason we need to forgive and let go. Forgiving and letting go does not absolve others of their part in the matter. That's something they will have to address, but it does clear you of any part you may have had in the situation.

Even if your part was simply holding a grudge, staying angry and upset, or wishing a mountain would fall on them. Holding onto negative feelings is just as harmful as committing a physical, negative act. You may think those thoughts are not really hurting anyone, but they are hurting you!

If you're still holding onto the villainous act performed against you, you are constantly reliving the pain of it! Every time you think about it your heart beats faster, your muscles tense up, you break out in a cold or hot sweat and your blood pressure rises.

You are wreaking havoc on your internal organs *and* that expansive outer one, your skin! Are you okay with taking meds to control your blood pressure, or acid blockers to ward off stomach ulcers? How about having to undergo plastic surgery to smooth out all the wrinkles, the dark puffy eye lids or those deep frown lines and folds your stressed-out skin will eventually develop?

I could be wrong, but I believe the best revenge is feeling *and* looking great during, and especially after someone has done their very best to cause you harm in some way.

But neither should you be resolved to rolling with the punches or counter blocking them either. That hurts! Instead, you should learn to do what I've termed the Muhammad Ali duck and dodge shuffle. When you sense a low blow coming your way, applying this technique doesn't get you hurt, *and* you'll look pretty in the process!

I have a free e-book that explains how to use this technique if you somehow find yourself in the ring with an opponent *instead* of the One. Look for those details at the end of the chapter.

Now that we've covered Biology and Phys Ed 101, let's get on with utilizing some empowering golden love nuggets! However, to save time, trees or your device's storage space, I will break these countdown reminders into six ten-second increments. Let's begin.

Note: The following is a scenario for the first meeting or date.

1-10 Second Mark: Before you start picking out wedding invitations remember, you don't know this person at all! You've just met, and it would be presumptuous or naive of you to leap to the probability of their oneness based on little-to-no information.

Even if they were at one time your high school sweetheart or crush, more than likely that was many, many, many moons ago. You probably didn't know them very well then and you still don't!

So, take a few deep cleansing breaths (preferably without looking or sounding like you're about to pass out) and simply see if you enjoy *talking* with them first or being in their space--their energy.

Try to keep the conversation light. Unless you're both atomic or molecular physicists, now is not the time to get too heavy or deep. The first date or meet up shouldn't include deciding when to meet parents, children, best friends or pets. Please leave them out of it for now!

Remember, you are no longer afraid of being passed over or rejected by anyone. As a matter of fact, you are so empowered now that you'd love for someone to decline getting to know you better.

Are you wondering why the heck would you love them to do such a thing? Well for one, they'd be doing you a *huge* favor. Letting you know sooner as opposed to much later that they are *not* what you desire to find in the One, will save you the time it will take to come to that very same conclusion.

They may not phrase it in this way, that they are not *your* best one, because not everyone will be honest or confident enough to admit that they are not the perfect match for you. But you can take their rejection or withdrawal to mean just that. As a matter of fact, you should thank them! In my opinion, not wasting anyone's time is time well spent.

10-20 Second Mark: Now that you two are engaging in light yet meaningful conversation, notice if they seem open, relaxed and paying attention to what is being said. Or do they seem nervous and constantly looking around as if waiting for the proverbial other shoe to drop...on their head!

Of course, you will take note of how you are responding and feeling as well. Are *you* being open, relaxed and paying attention or are you feeling a bit uneasy, doubtful or nervous while communicating with them?

Note: I'm not referring to the uneasy feeling of wondering if your hair looks like you just stuck a wet finger into a live socket. Or if a piece of green lettuce is dangling between your front teeth.

If it seems the communication is lacking something or you're not feeling much of anything at all, ask yourself why you are feeling the way that you do. Then wait, listen, watch or feel for the answer, but never accept an answer that is based in fear. It could be you're feeling a bit insecure because you think you're not interesting enough and that you may seem boring to them.

However, since they didn't doze off while you were in mid-sentence, or their eyes remained focused and didn't glaze over like someone with a very bad concussion, you're probably not boring them.

Being boring isn't something to worry about. If you are both open and relaxed, just keep talking and see where it leads. On the other hand, should the conversation take an uncomfortable turn, be aware of it. Do not brush it off as your imagination or nervousness.

Do they seem too pushy, anxious and nervous, *or* are they're jumping over, crawling under and skirting completely around topic? Then that yellow caution light should be alerting you to pay even closer attention.

Is there no follow-up, do they take long pauses before responding? *Or* are they giving you an answer before you can complete a question? Do they seem in awe of their phone because it's constantly lighting up like a Christmas tree? If so, then things have moved past yellow to almost red alert. But you still have a few options at your disposal.

1. Politely excuse yourself and walk away.
2. Give them more time to redeem *or* reveal themselves.

Note: It could be that something stressful is occurring in their life and they're anticipating good or unfortunate news. Or it's quite possible that they may be extremely nervous or shy and not actually stepping out on a significant other they forgot to mention.

However, unless them being rude, evasive, extremely nervous or shy is on your must-have list, then it is okay for you to move on. But before you take the high road, ask more detailed questions *without* grilling them like Elliot Ness.

Check in with your feelings and you'll be better able to sense if they are simply dealing with something unrelated to the act of deception, having the first date jitters or exhibiting latent character traits you have no interest whatsoever in dealing with!

20-30 Second Mark: There's nothing like a sincere compliment. But if you are inundated with one's concerning the herringbone pattern of your jacket, the wave of your hair, the heel taps on your shoes, your car key emblem, cell phone case and your flawless manicure, it could be that their flattery knows no bounds. *Or* they're sizing you up against *their* unique list!

Whichever it is, this type of over-the-top flattery should lead you to consider what their true intentions may be. At the least, it should draw attention to their unusual social and conversational skills. Again, calmly follow your gut and the way to proceed will be made evident. On the other hand, if they're asking engaging questions that will encourage deeper dialogue like:

"How do you feel about dating exclusively? What do you like to do to relax and unwind? Do you have a favorite book (movie or place to visit)? Are you a dog or cat person?"

If they are also answering your questions without hesitation or reserve, then you know what to do in this case too. Continue to engage but remember, you have all the time in the world. So, there's no reason to rush and leap to any conclusions.

You're no longer coming from a place of fear but of empowerment. Just keep engaging and learning more about them while staying within your most comfortable rhythm and flow.

30-40 Second Mark: Woo-Hoo! You've made it to the half-way mark! Apparently, they have some redeeming qualities, or you would have been out of there by now. Hopefully at this point in your awareness, you know it's not beneficial for either party to be led on or used just to ward off boredom or loneliness. That's what hobbies and pets are for, not people.

I won't go gangsta' priestess on you, but that old familiar adage, *"Treat others the way you want to be treated"* is a golden nugget we should all adhere to. Don't play games, lie or conveniently hide critical information. Of course, if *you're* okay with being played, lied to and later discovering your fabulous one surgically changed their gender five years ago and somehow "forgot" to inform you of it, then continue playing the games and telling the lies. This is just a head's up, and I am not accusing or judging anyone *but* doing that kind of stuff can seriously mess up a person's head and life!

You must know that game players are never given full immunity or exempt from the inevitable fallout their well-executed game moves create. In some shape, form or fashion, what you put out there eventually comes right back at ya'!

40-50 Second Mark: Now you can begin considering how or when to take things to the next level. By next level I mean the next date. Here I go sounding just like a broken record again. Whether I sound like a scathed record or not, you don't, and you can say this along with me if you like. Here comes your part:

"I don't really know them yet!"

Acknowledging this fact is not some outdated platitude, it's being smart! Better than that, it demonstrates emotional strength and rock-solid character. You're no longer in the business of being a people pleaser *unless* what you are doing pleases you first!

Don't worry, it doesn't mean you're being selfish when placing your desires first. It simply means you are courageous enough; love yourself enough to consider your own state of happiness. Short of suffering from a self-defeating masochistic disorder, why would anyone choose to be miserable first?

Again, no one can make another "feel" love or happiness any more than they can make someone see or understand. The act of experiencing and expressing *any* level of awareness, emotion or thought will always be an inside job.

50-60 Second Mark: You've both made it to the last seconds together. That's quite an accomplishment. Some marriages don't last that long! For real, I kid you not. However, it can take time, maybe even years to truly "know" a person. However, by now you have the utmost confidence in knowing yourself.

You know what you want, and you also know what your responsibilities are. That being, to love and nourish yourself *first*. In this way others who are so inclined, whether they are the One, family or friends, coworkers, complete strangers or the big Rottweiler next door, they will follow where ever your love leads them to.

I don't think I can ring this bell enough times, but one of the most important things you can accomplish in your life is to know and love yourself. Think about this. Wouldn't it be ridiculous to expect someone to know more about you than you do, or to love and care for you more than you do? Exactly!

Now you have it, your very own personal means for experiencing the love you desire. But you should experience love every single day of your life, and you should do so whether Mr. or Ms. Right is in the mist of it.

Never limit yourself when it comes to love. There's just so much of it out there to be experienced! I'm sure you know that expressing and experiencing love isn't limited to two people. And no, I am *not* talking about being a player. Remember, we don't play with people's emotions because we don't want our emotions played with.

What I'm referring to is being a lover of life! Wouldn't you have much more fun in life if you love what you do to earn a living? What about becoming a lover of learning new and interesting things? I'm referring to those things that will challenge you and help you grow or just be fun to do!

Imagine how much more enjoyable life will be if you love your home environment, or how you spend your leisure time. Wouldn't you love co-creating with other like-minded individuals, sharing your talents, experiencing new foods, arts, crafts and hobbies or visiting new and interesting places?

You may even find that most of these new and exciting things are right in your own backyard! Variety is truly the spice of life, don't you agree? The potential for experiencing something new every single day *and* loving it is astronomical!

So, have fun stretching your known limits and be adventurous sometimes, experiment a bit. Not everything or everyone you experience will result in an instant love for you. But you don't have to hate those things or people either. They will be what they will be. However, you have the option to wallow or not to wallow in what they be!

While it seems much easier to love or feel neutral about a thing that cannot possibly love us back, we usually have a problem with applying that same ease of love or neutrality when it comes to people.

Just remember that when dealing with people who seem difficult to like--let alone love, it is not your responsibility to make them loveable! Stay true to being you and move on from the experience without hating. In this way, you'll have no regrets. Moving on while being hate and regret free means you truly have nothing but love for yourself *and* for them. You'll be okay, even if they don't love you back!

Also, don't forget to let your creative juices flow! Don't get caught up in the daily, humdrum grind of it all. That's not living, that's just biding time! Here's another thought.

While you are enjoying and loving the life you're living, you are bound to run into Mr. or Miss Right, aka the "One!" How so you ask? For one, they will be doing some of the same things you will be doing in your pursuit of happiness. And you know what they say about birds of a feather. They usually flock together and end up sitting on the same roost!

Second, remember that glow of confidence, love and authenticity I mentioned earlier? Well, aside from the occasional PoPo's curiosity of the fully luminous, awesomely engaged and aware you, you will begin attracting more like minds and hearts. Now, I'm not saying every like mind-heart individual you meet will be the love of your life, but they may be the perfect fit for other needs.

They can either be a best friend, business partner, creative muse, mentor or advisor. Need I go on? No, I'm sure you can take it from here. So, leap out of that starting gate and hook up with that awesome One! You two deserve each other.

Hum…are you *still* here? You do know you're burning daylight, right? Come on, you've got this! Just slip on your Super Being suit and turn on your light so the One can see *you* in all your glory!

Have fun!

AFTERWORD

I've had so much fun sharing these insights with you, and I'd be tickled pink to know ~~if~~ *when* you've hooked up with the One by incorporating any of the life lessons I've included in this book. These lessons are by no means new and improved for today's seeker of the One.

On the contrary, they are as old as love itself. As a matter of fact, I believe the life lessons we encounter are designed to prepare us for the wealth of knowledge and awareness that is already encoded within our DNA. We simply didn't know it was possible to gain access to all that knowledge!

The things I've asked you to consider may feel like an innovative approach to love because we've been advised to do a lot of unproductive things. Like jumping through flaming hoops just to impress someone (and being singed or seriously burned for our efforts), changing or upgrading the way we look, enhancing our marketability (as if we're a product with limited shelf life) and employing a few tricks to lure or hook another individual.

But none of these laborious efforts are required. You only need to get and stay in touch with the *real* you, figure out what you desire to experience, and then love staying true to being you!

That's it in a nutshell folks! Don't overdo or over think the process, you'll only complicate things. Just ease into your greatness! Okay? Oh, and don't forget, if you happen to hook up with the "One" after reading my book and applying any of the life lessons and golden love nuggets we talked about, please let me know! I want to hear all about it. Well, maybe not *all* your business, but as much as you're willing to share with me.

Until next time, keep growing and know that you can only go where your heart, head and feet take you. So, maintain a light and happy heart, hold onto the best of thoughts and always wear comfortable shoes!

Enjoy!

ABOUT THE AUTHOR

Yvonne L. Jones is a native of Houston, Texas. She is an Inspirational Life Ambassador in training and the author of another insightful how-to book, *How To Strengthen Your Gut, Lose The "But" And Live Your Life Regret Free* as well as two books of poetry, *At The River's Edge Where Quantum Streams Flow* and *Speaking Out And Listening In.*

For information about the author, new books and audio release dates, the benefits of becoming a VIP reader or to grab your **free** relationship e-book visit:
https://lsbpublishing.com/contact

If you have enjoyed this Little Sepia Book, please take just a moment and give it an honest review at:
https://amazon.com/author/yvonne

Thank You!

Made in the USA
Coppell, TX
20 December 2021